GABRIELLA LEWENZ

GABRIELLA LEWENZ

Published 18 February 2016

Jackson House Publishing Company

40 Motukaha Road
Waiheke Island, New Zealand

ISBN 978-0-47312278-2

Printed in USA

Most works in this book are in private collections

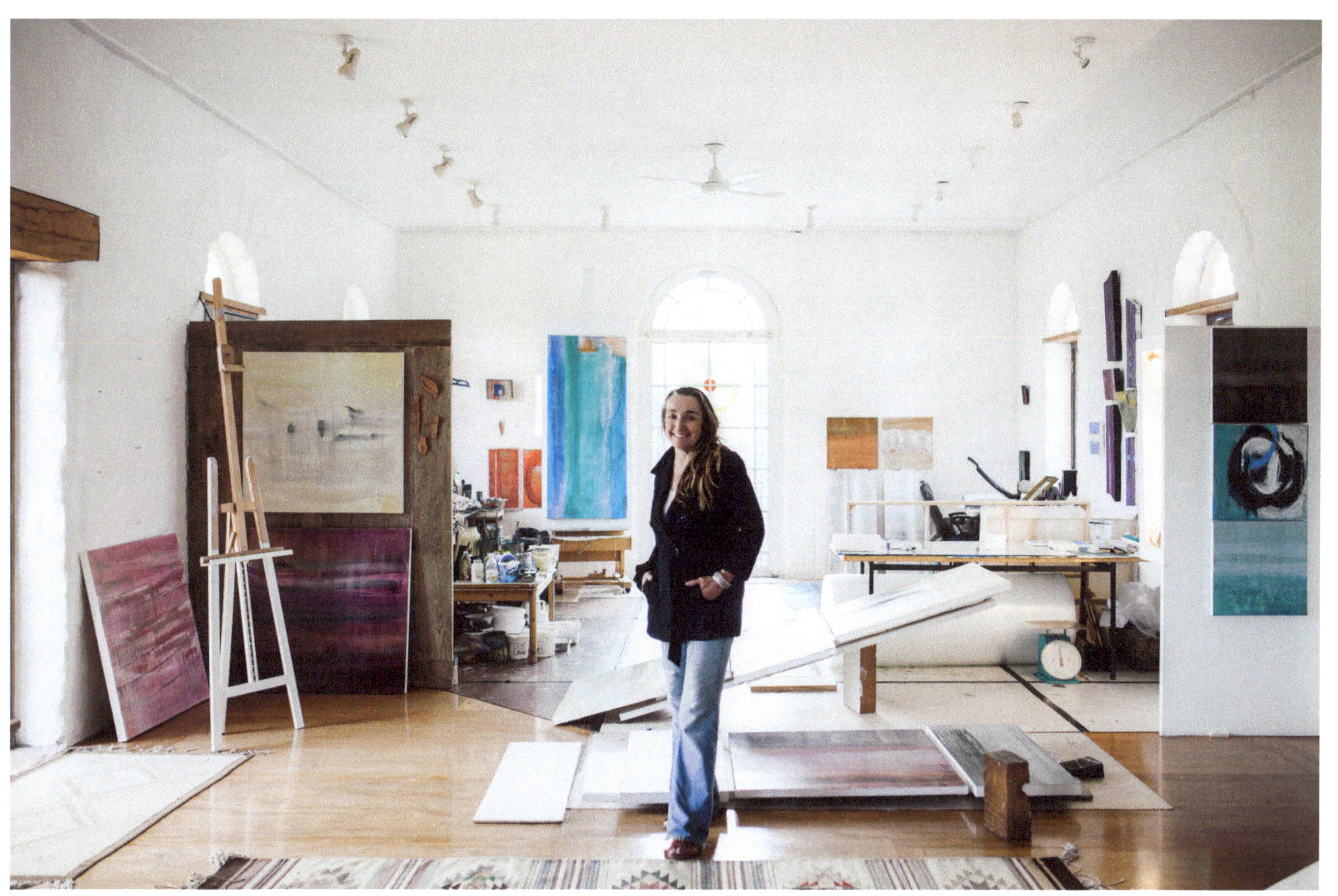

Story - An interview with Gabriella

Born in Greece of American diplomat parents, Gabriella's first language was Greek – a language lost when her family moved to Pakistan and then at age 12, due to her father's terminal illness, to America, leaving her only with English as a second language. As a result of her unusual upbringing she finds her form of expression is not so much in words, but goes directly from impression to paint.

Patrons want to know the story – the words that explain her works. Her buyers have an immediate, intuitive response to the works of art. They get it, they feel it, yet embedded in a culture of words, often need to hear the story in words.

One evening with clear intent to find Gabriella's story – to translate it from the etheric to the articulate, a narrative emerged for this book and an upcoming show.

What happens when you go into the studio?

I begin to search.

Search for what?

I begin to search for an opening to the painting. It's more like I step into a darkness in approaching and starting a new work. Inspiration is found there in that dark space, yet often hard to access. It doesn't come easy. I'm aware of my physical and emotional density as I begin to work through the process; of doubt, of the unknown, and questioning. Shifting my focus from my head to connect with my heart, I begin to search through this portal for a certain quality in the painting, a quality which can transform through the many layers of oils onto the surface. There is a presence felt through colour. Colour transforms.

My experience is often about being alone… not a loneliness, but a certain sharp awareness of aloneness. This space I begin to break through within the work. I base everything on observation. This requires to dig deep inside this chaotic, unorganised potential to search for the light and transitions within the painting. The painting is the quest to become light again, through the fields of colour and contrasts of extremes. With each new painting I aim for this search – again and again.

As I begin to paint, I shift into a different state; I don't think about the painting process. I let forms come, light and colour interact. I don't plan what will emerge, yet later I can see it's based on the forces around me. Rangitoto, the volcano to the west; the ever-changing sea shaped by a forceful climate: wind, rain, then sudden, brilliant sun.

Other forces are timeless, as in a childhood memory when my family was leaving Greece, a fisherman gave my father an ancient urn fished up in his net. That amphora has become an iconic reference in my work. The vessel, a metaphor for this profound gifting, is echoed in many of my paintings.

When I went to Italy for a three months art residency, the paintings changed from the rich layered colours of Waiheke Island to the etheric, thin washes of an ancient land with a very different spirit – as if the veil had thinned over thousand of years of human presence. Italy challenged me as I had to start with an empty studio… no paint, no brushes, no mediums to start with. Heading to the art store in Lecce was a delight. They sold small flat wood pegs made to secure canvas frames. I thought to paint on them as part of my doodling practice; a process I often begin before I face a blank canvas. These are my 'ink narratives' notebooks, an ongoing series with ink and gouache. When the art critic for La Republica came to my studio, he loved them and insisted I include them in my show.

When I returned to Waiheke Island to resume my work, the paintings captured the light, translucence of the fire, water and air of the island and its volcanic landscape bursting out of the sea.

How do you work?

I work on three or more paintings at a given time. As I said, I start with a sensation of my own density, and the process can be very difficult. It is hard to find the openings, it does not just come. The painting evolves.

What is the feeling as the light comes?

I feel lighter, a joy. I'm aware of working from the inside out, beginning to navigate through the senses of my heart. I feel the painting. There are a million different directions to take to make a painting happen. Each painting is a different journey. Some may not work and I give up on them for a while. I set those paintings aside and it can take years before I go back to them and resume the search. I never lay down a white surface over an unfinished work. I use the old layers as a backdrop; under the surface the old layers are still there, like the redemption of the journey of life, giving more texture, richness and in its own way, light.

[As the interview progresses, Gabriella commented…] I did not realise how painful it was, this density - that is the human condition - and how strongly this presents itself when I begin a work. My paintings are a way for me to leave the pain; it is a search to return home.

When you create a trilogy, is it one painting from the onset; is it one search?

After a number of panels or canvases are complete I then explore ways of combining the works into a trilogy, to create visual narratives, and at times creating beautiful tensions between each panel. Many of my works are triptychs. I started working with a form of three panel works based on my childhood visits to the Greek Orthodox churches in Thessaloniki, and outer islands; a three-hinged panel that sit on an alter rather than hung on the wall. The works are not religious in the manner of the old icons, but they are going toward the light, toward the etheric elements in the landscapes.

When the paintings are done, what do you feel?

I want them to go out into the world. I want to release them. The greatest feeling is selling them. When, sometimes years later, the buyer reports the joy it brings into their life, it confirms that my process of working has a deeper value beyond just creating a 'lovely piece' with beautiful colour. The paintings carries an essence, what in Maori is called 'wairua' or spirit, long after I finish the work. I like to think of my paintings as totemic in their feel. Recently, an American publisher asked if they could reproduce a work of mine. This work happened to be a commission. Unlike works sold off the wall, commissioned works passes copyright to the buyer. So I contacted the buyer, and they replied the painting was very special to them, too special for reproductions. I would never have heard that if the publisher had not seen the image on my web site and asked about it.

So it brings light into peoples lives?

To feel one's aloneness can be daunting, and it can be freeing as well.

I'm reminded of a child in the wilderness alone, in a process of trusting in which directions to go. There are no guarantees. It can be terrifying on a deep level, and my search can feel that way on canvas. When the buyer purchases a painting – either out of the gallery or commissioned, they bring that journey into the light, into their homes… which may be why the paintings mean so much to them.

So, to answer your question, yes I think my paintings do carry light into people's lives.

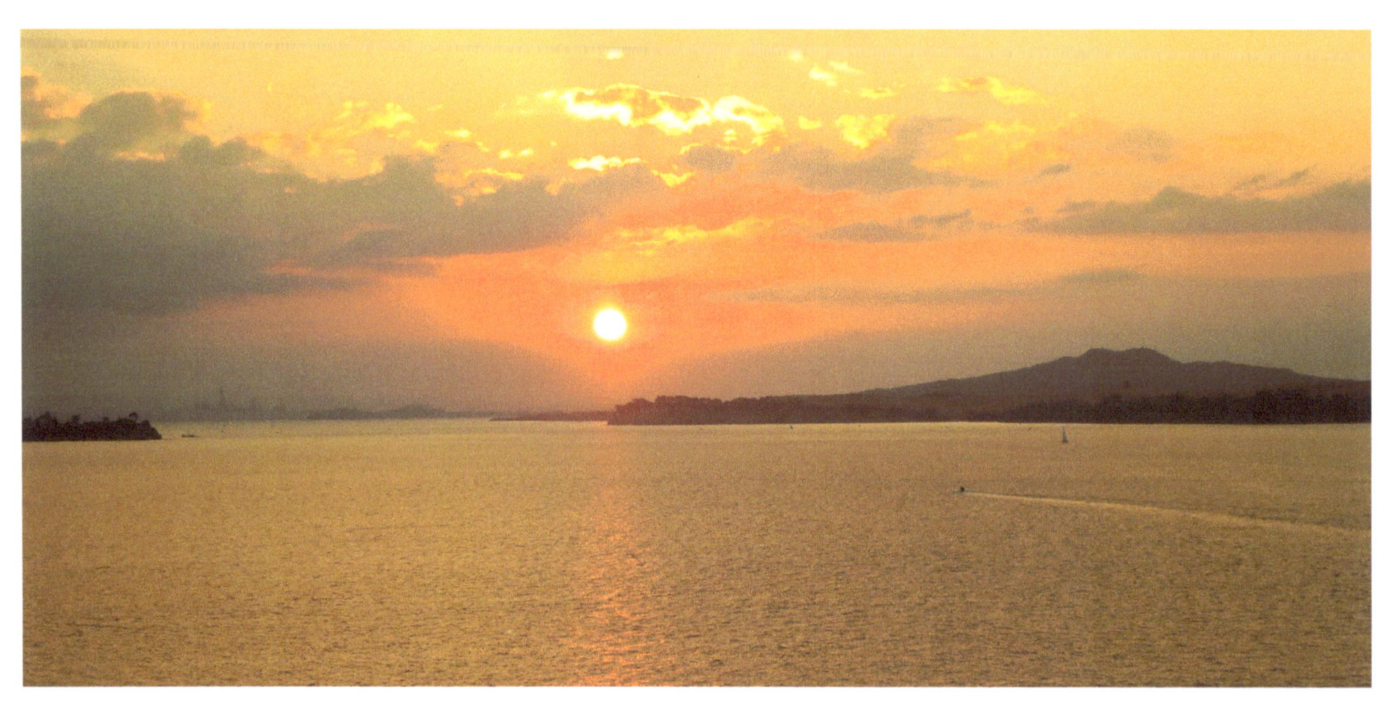

'Rangitoto Shimmering' - crossing the channel to waiheke island you pass a dormant volcanic landscape 'Rangitoto'

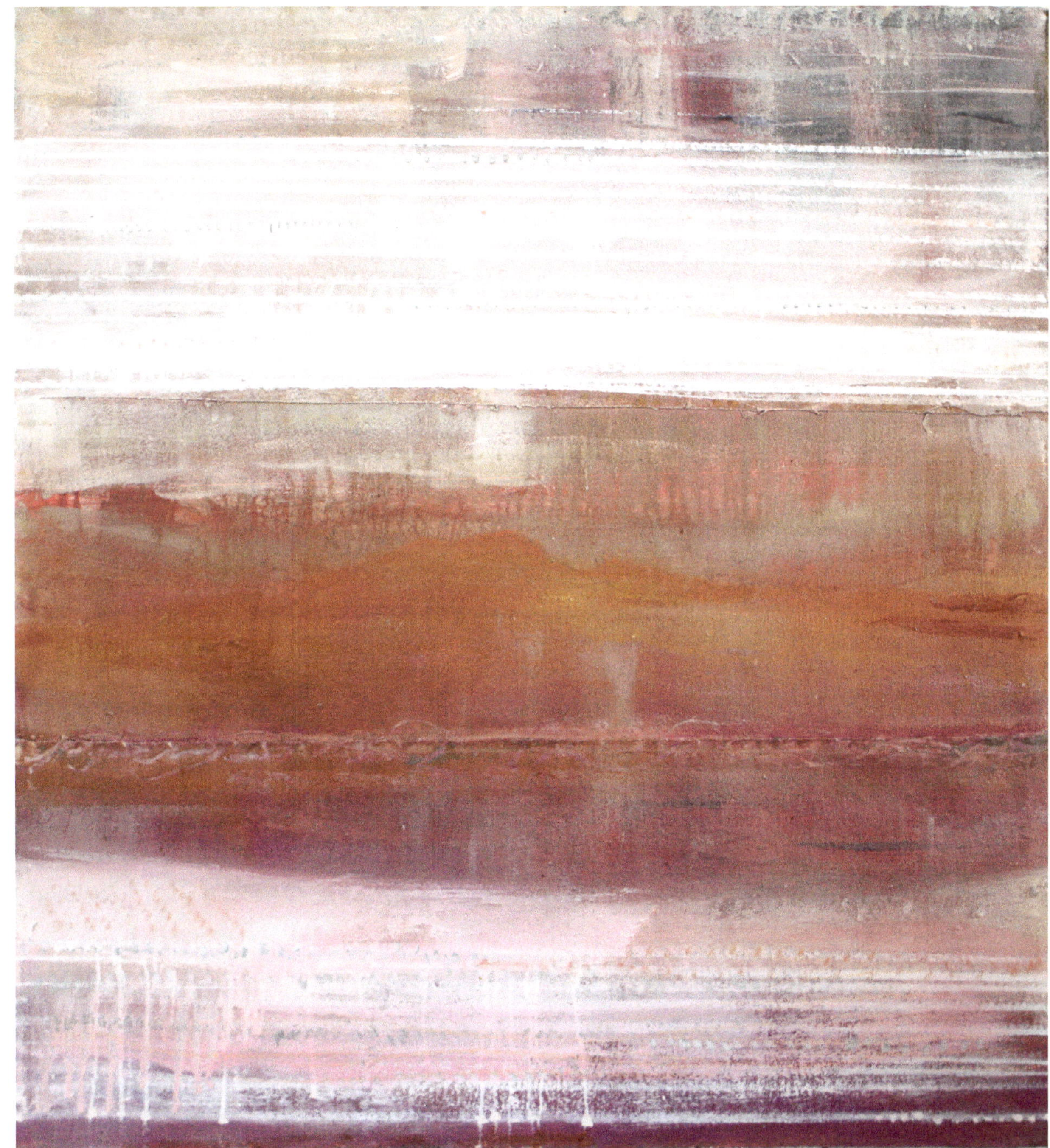

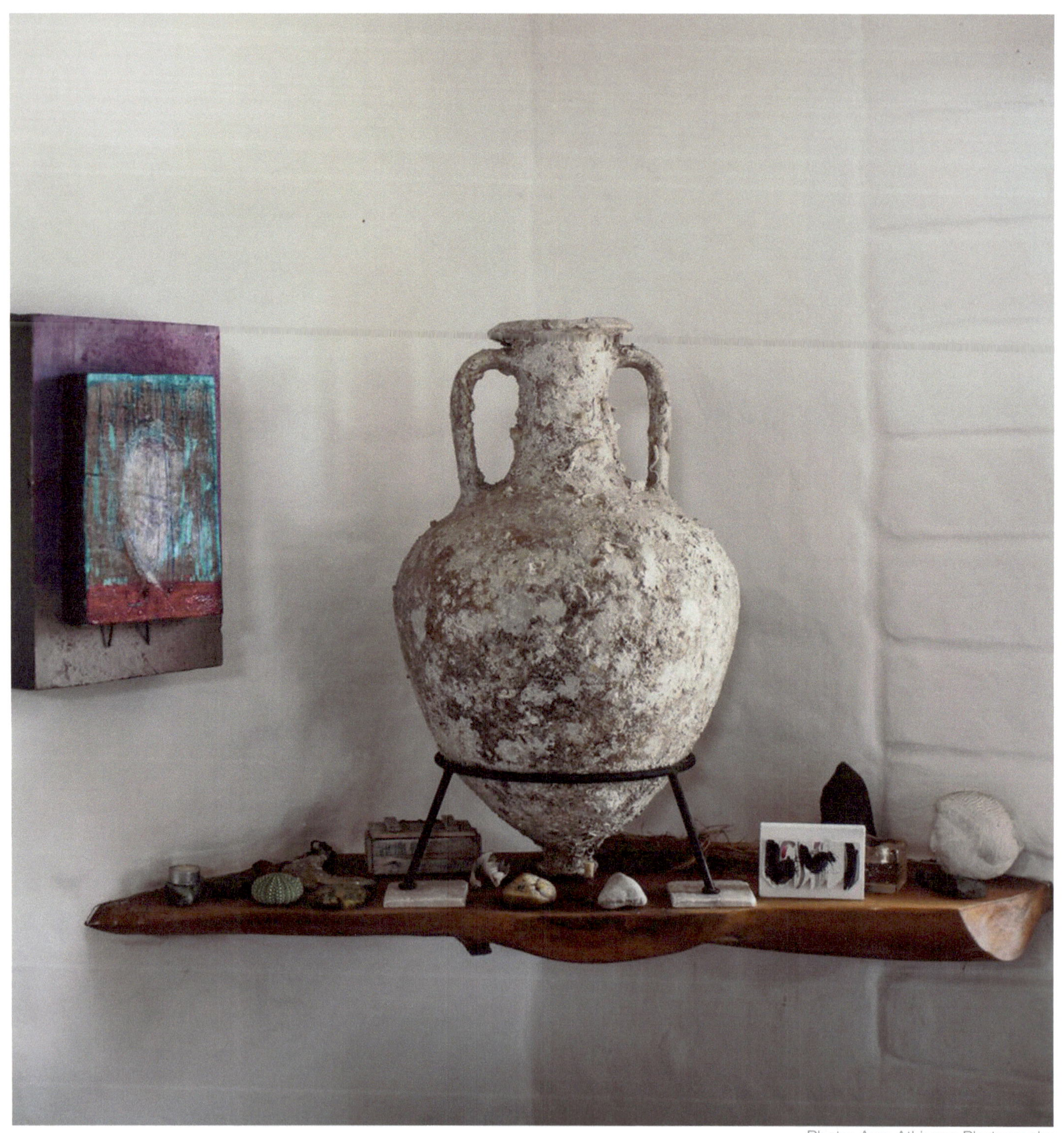

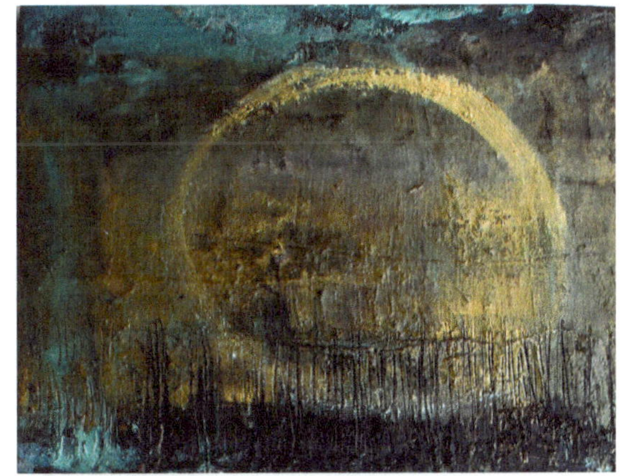

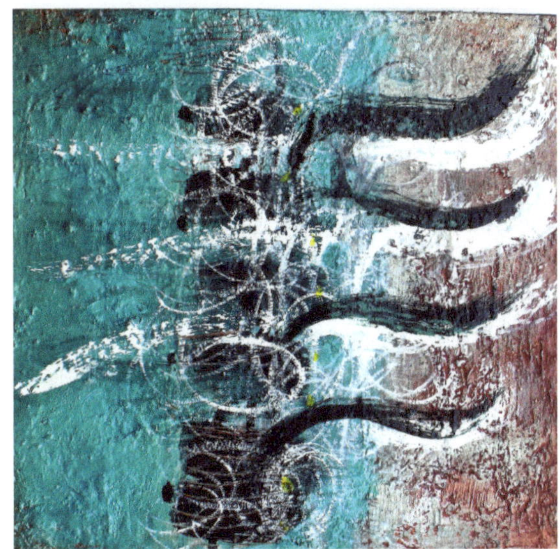

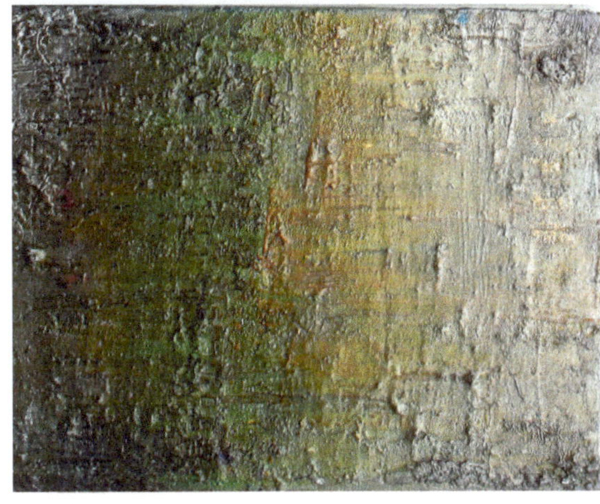

Ocean Dance Rhapsody

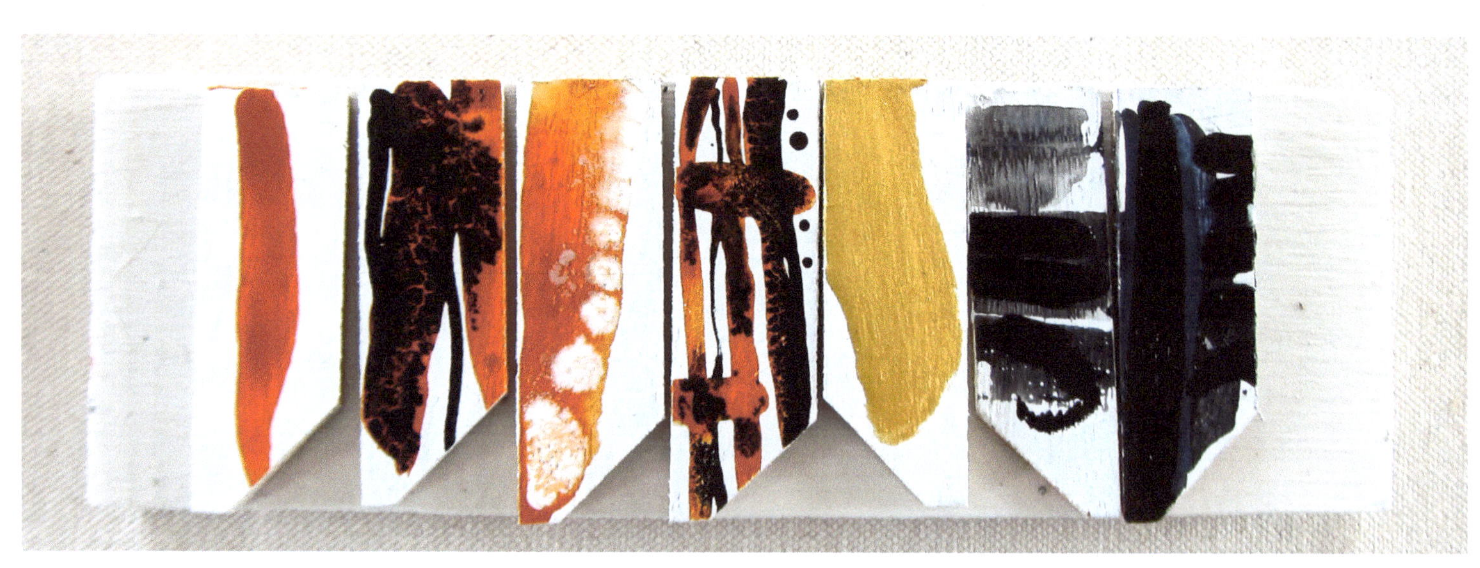

Ink Narratives 'Tempo' on display at Palazzo Palmieri . FRANTOIO IPOGEO, Martignano Italy

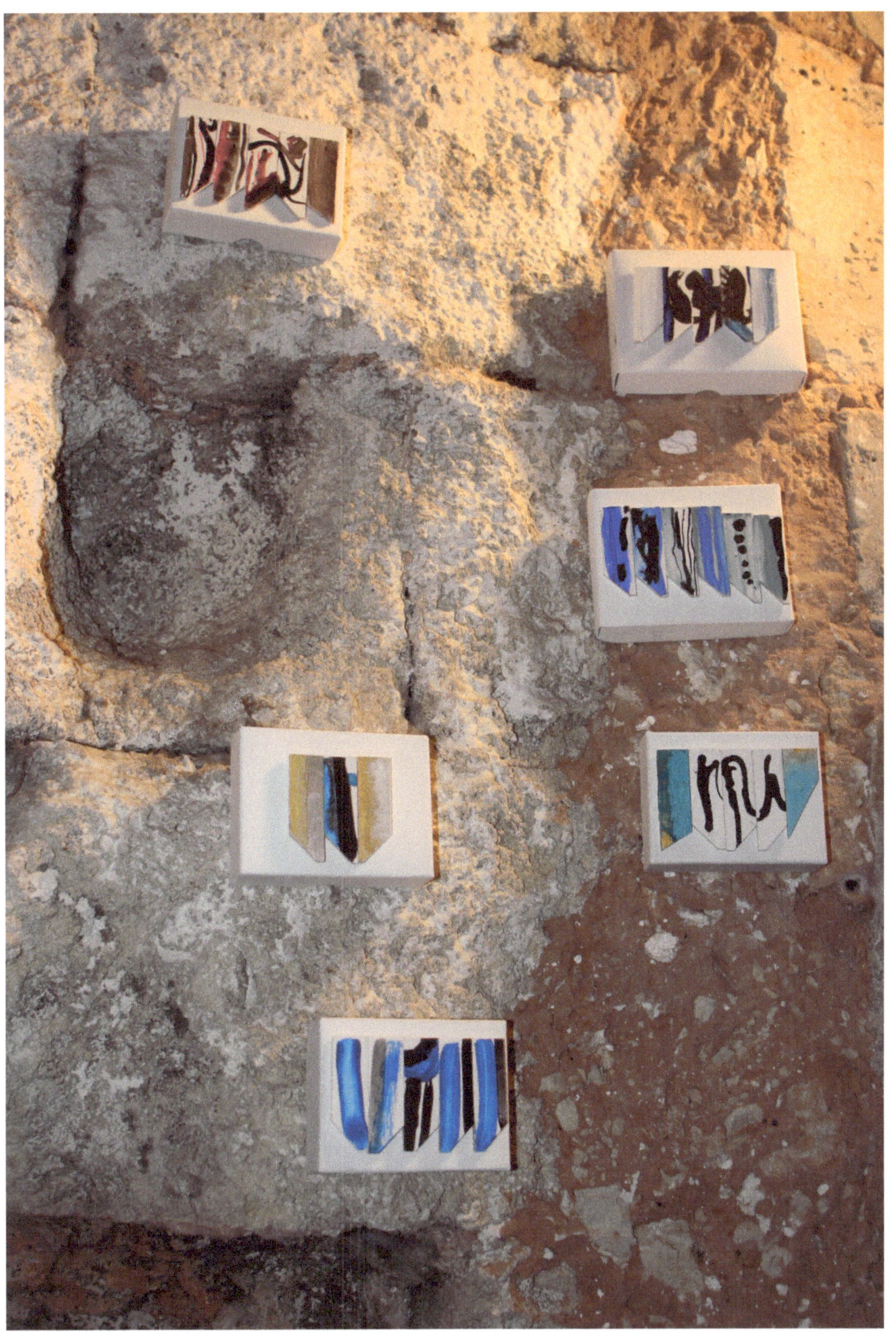

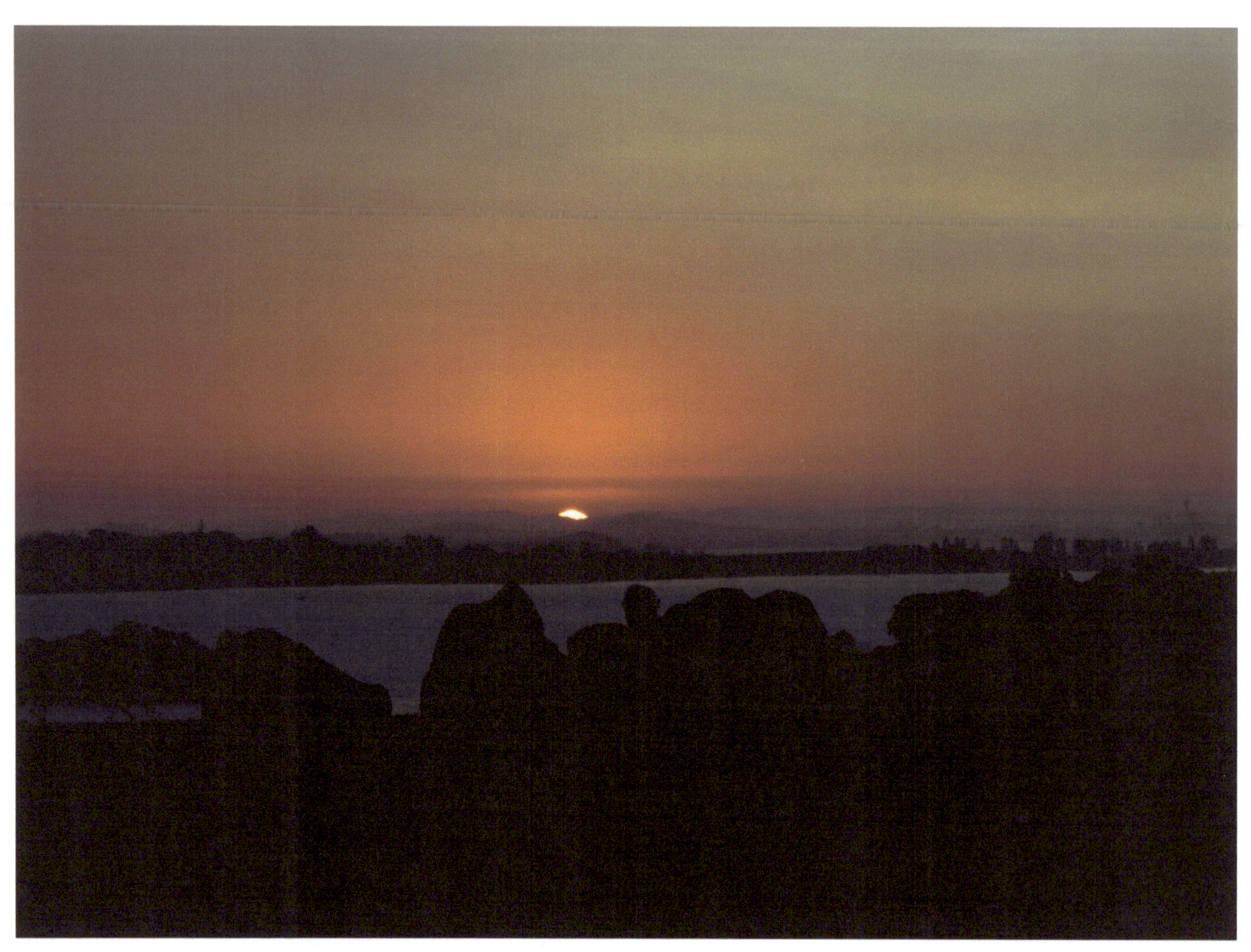

'Portal Harmony Teals'

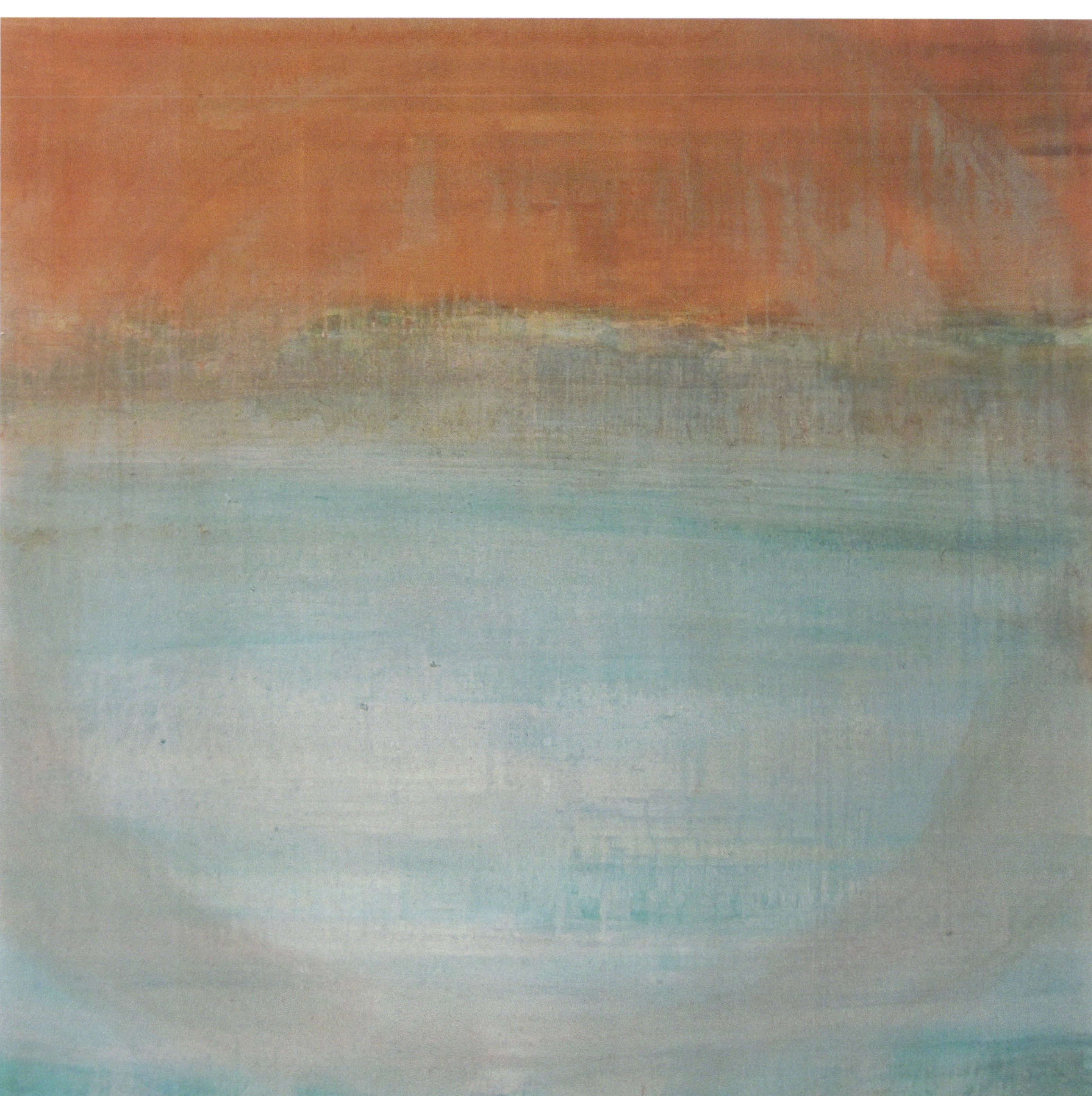

A Round of Hope.

Sun lowers
the second cycle of the day,
a primer
of shadows and light.
And a sharpness wraps onto land,
the elements
like a tincture
ripening the day
before the night begins.
Between trees - a turning cycle of earth.

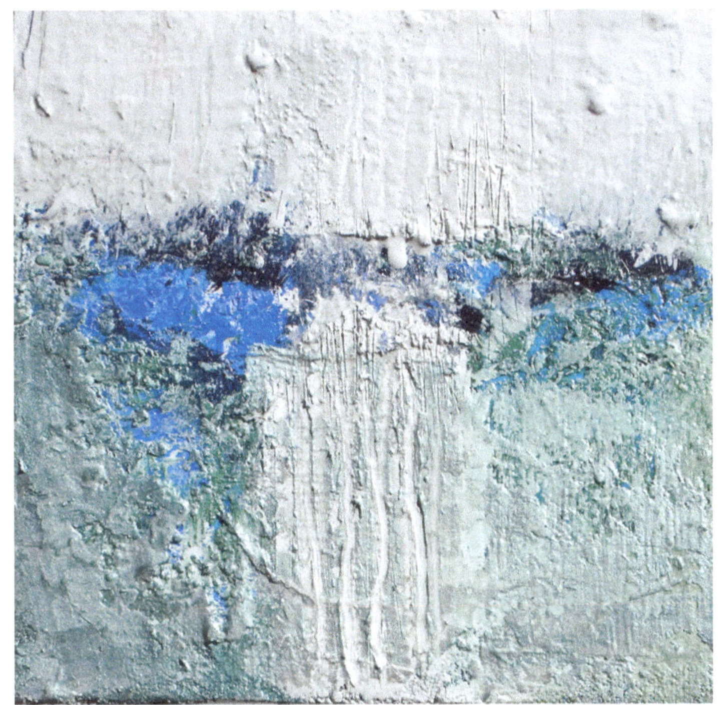

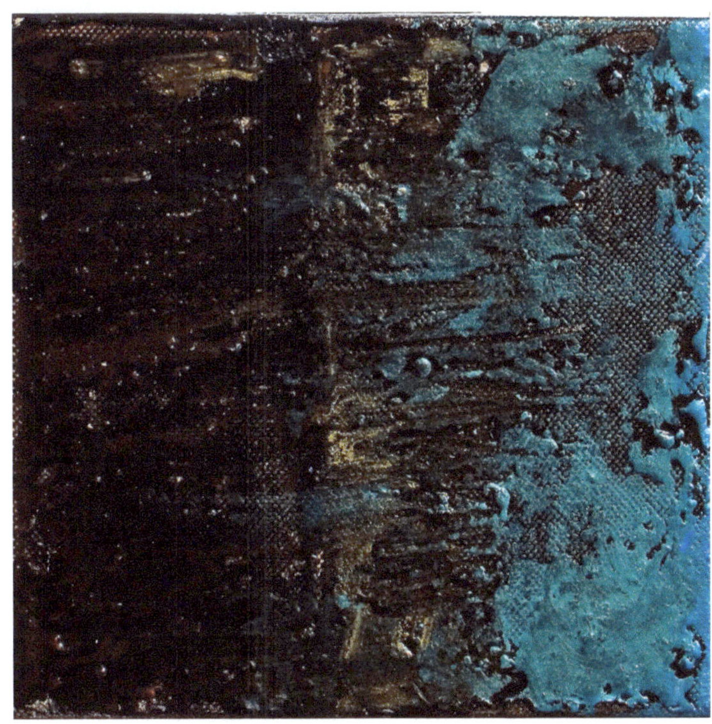

'White Falls'

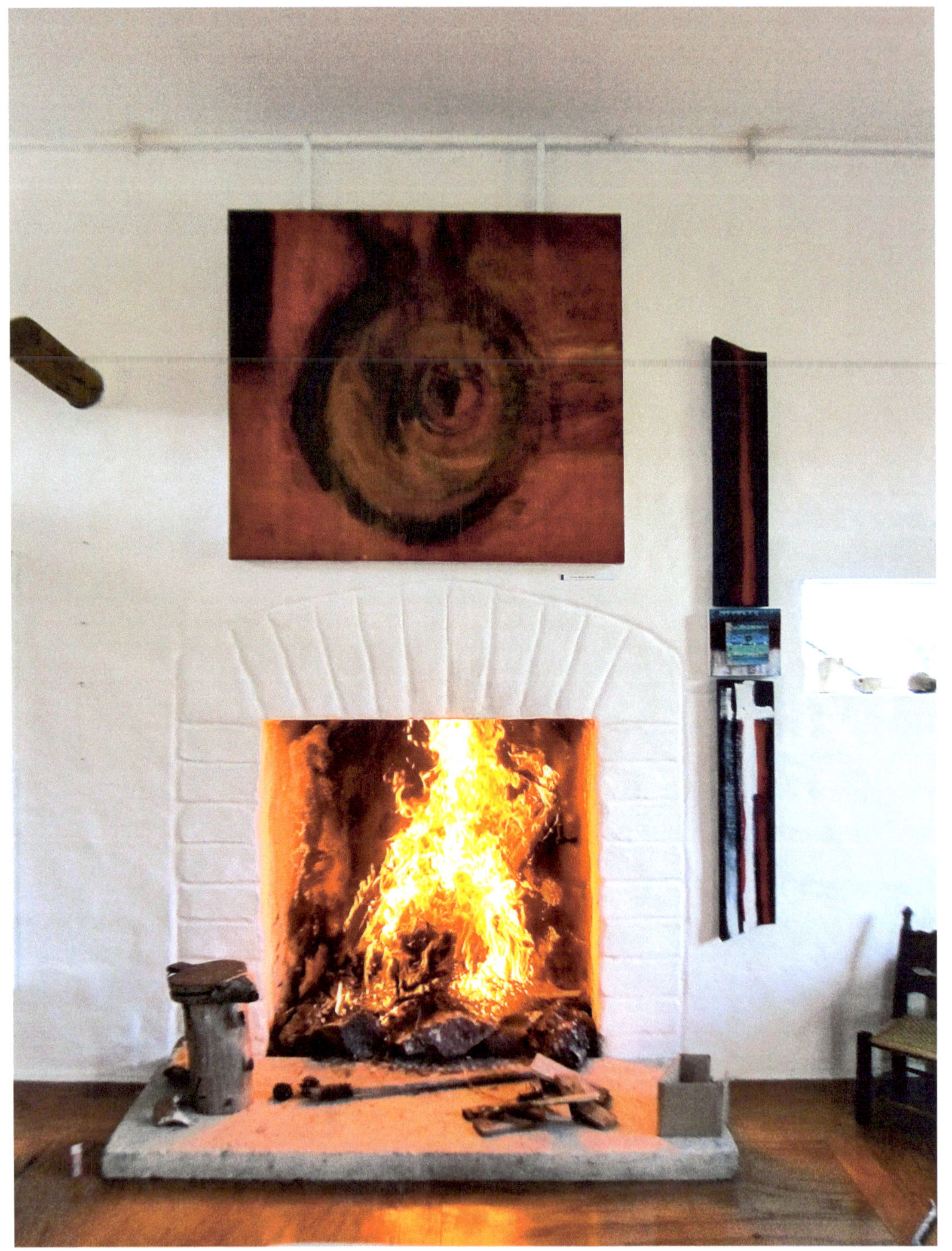

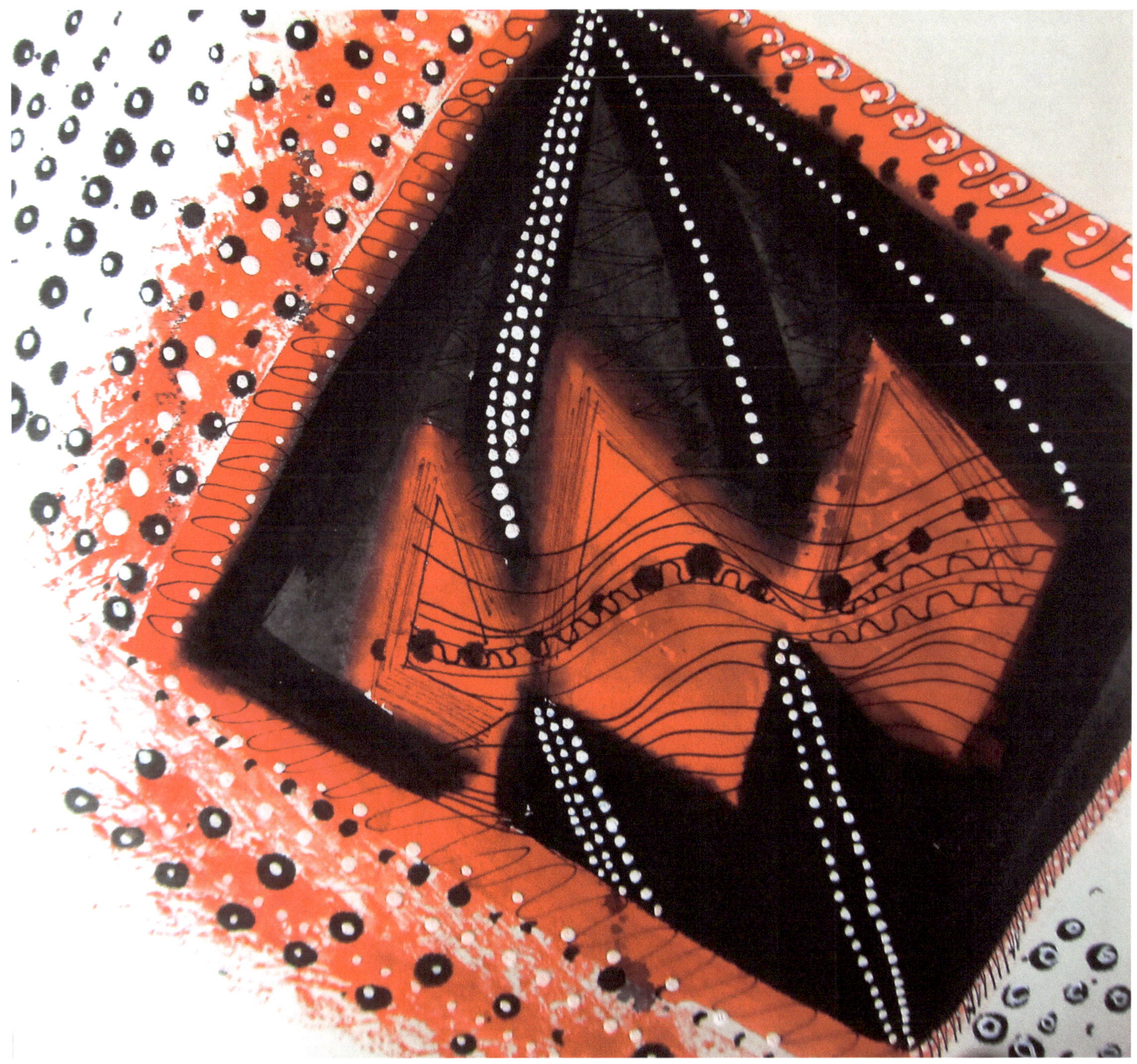

Ink Narratives series

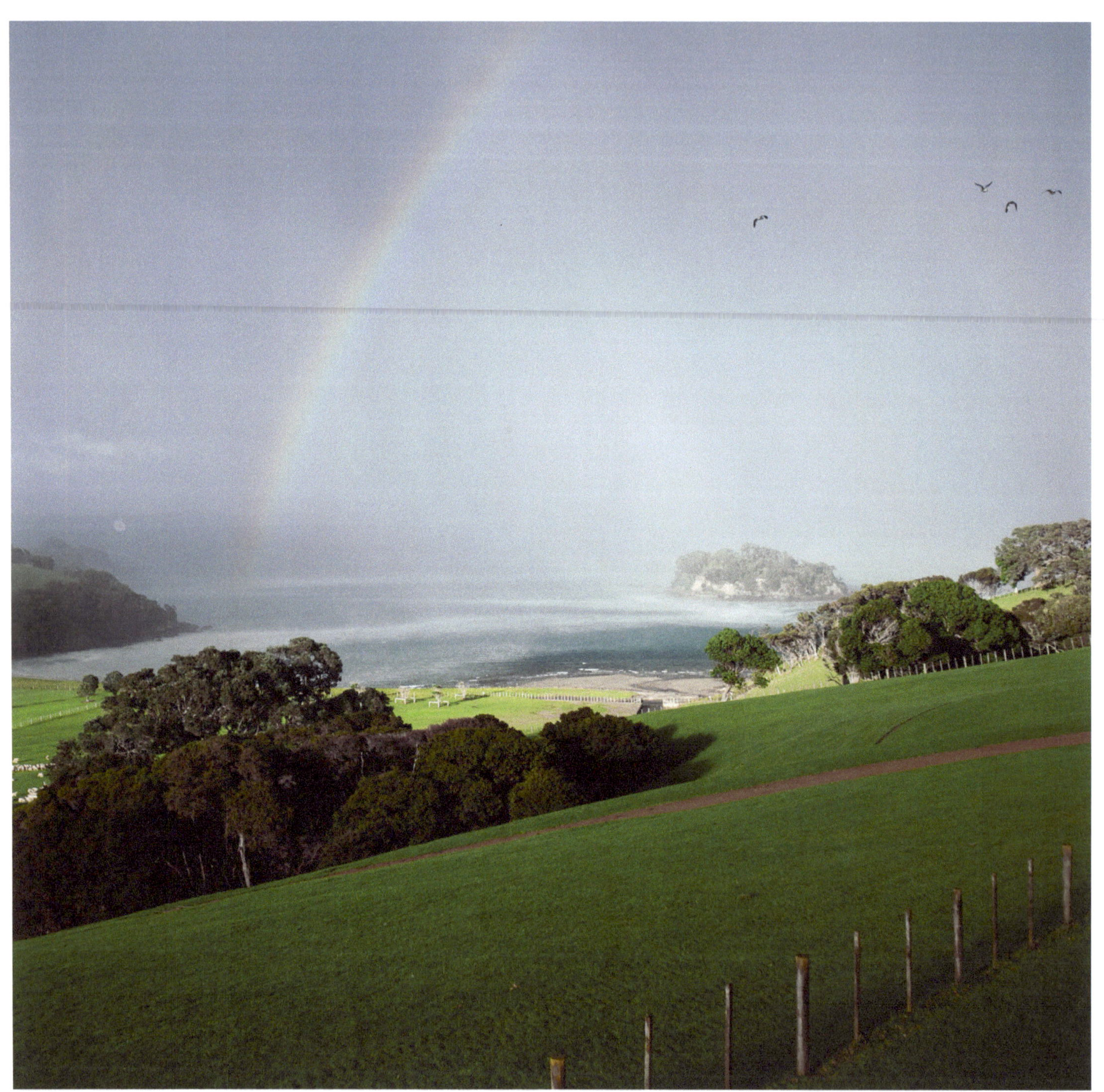

View from the studio over Motukaha Island

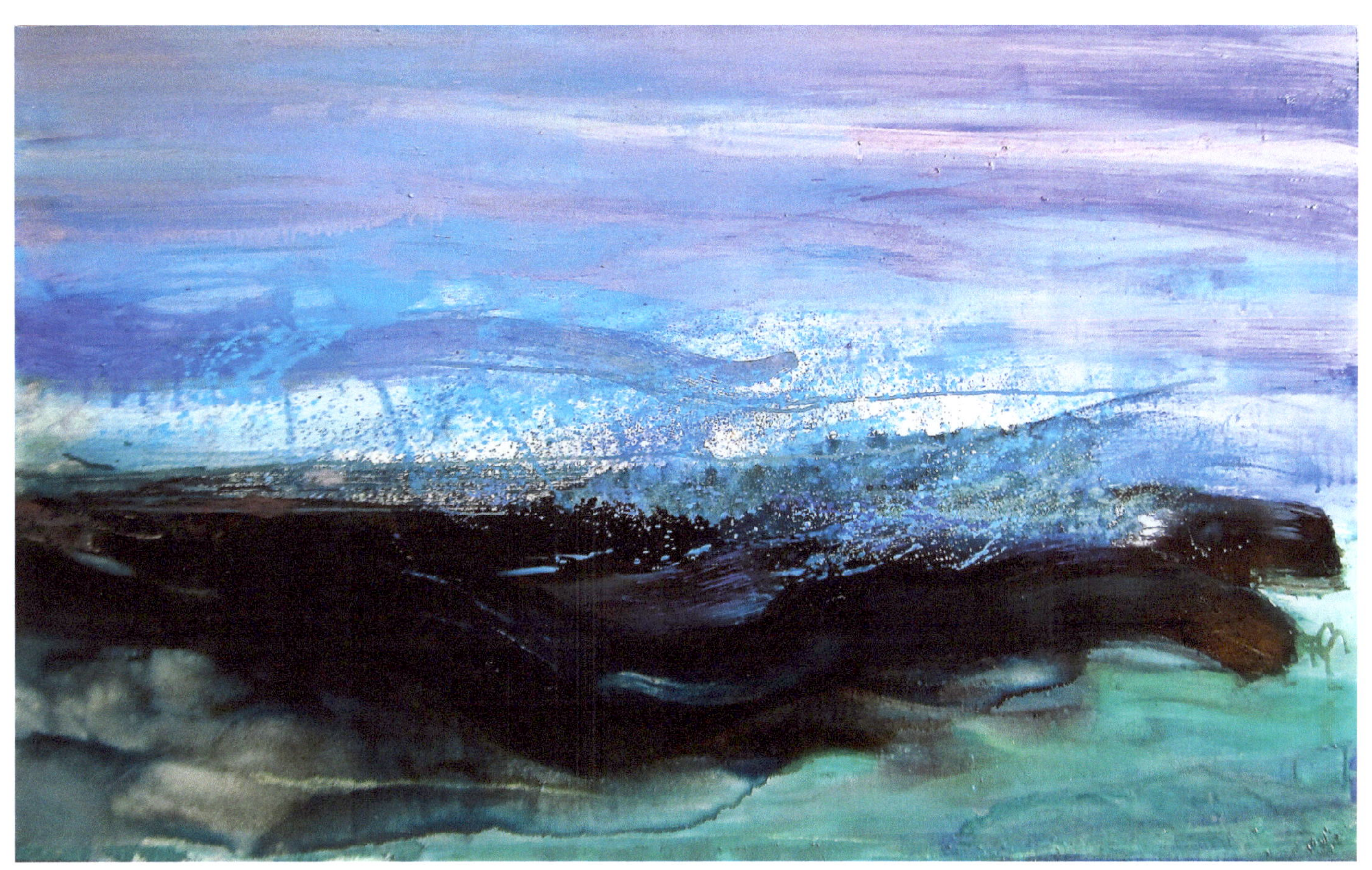

'Ocean Surge'

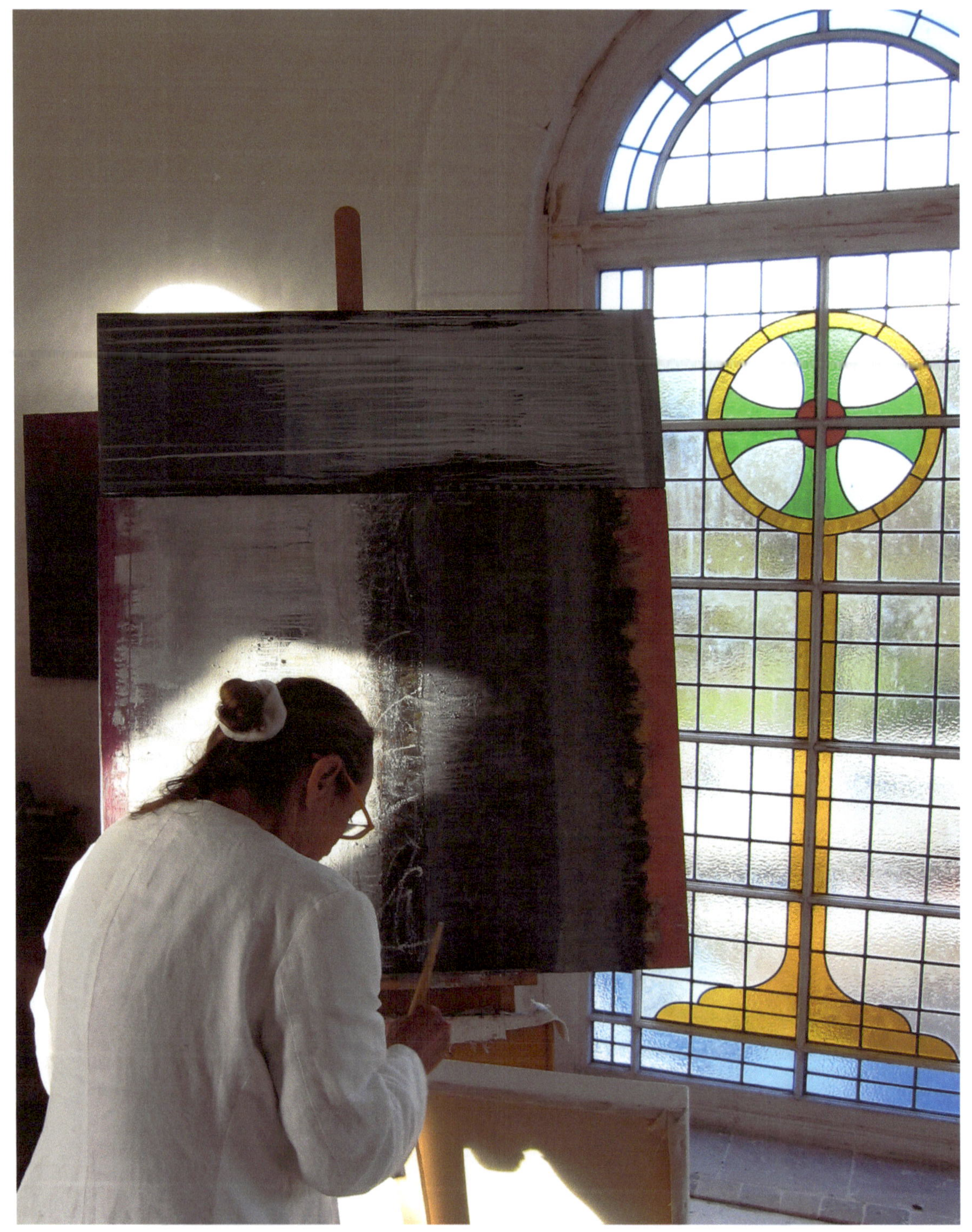

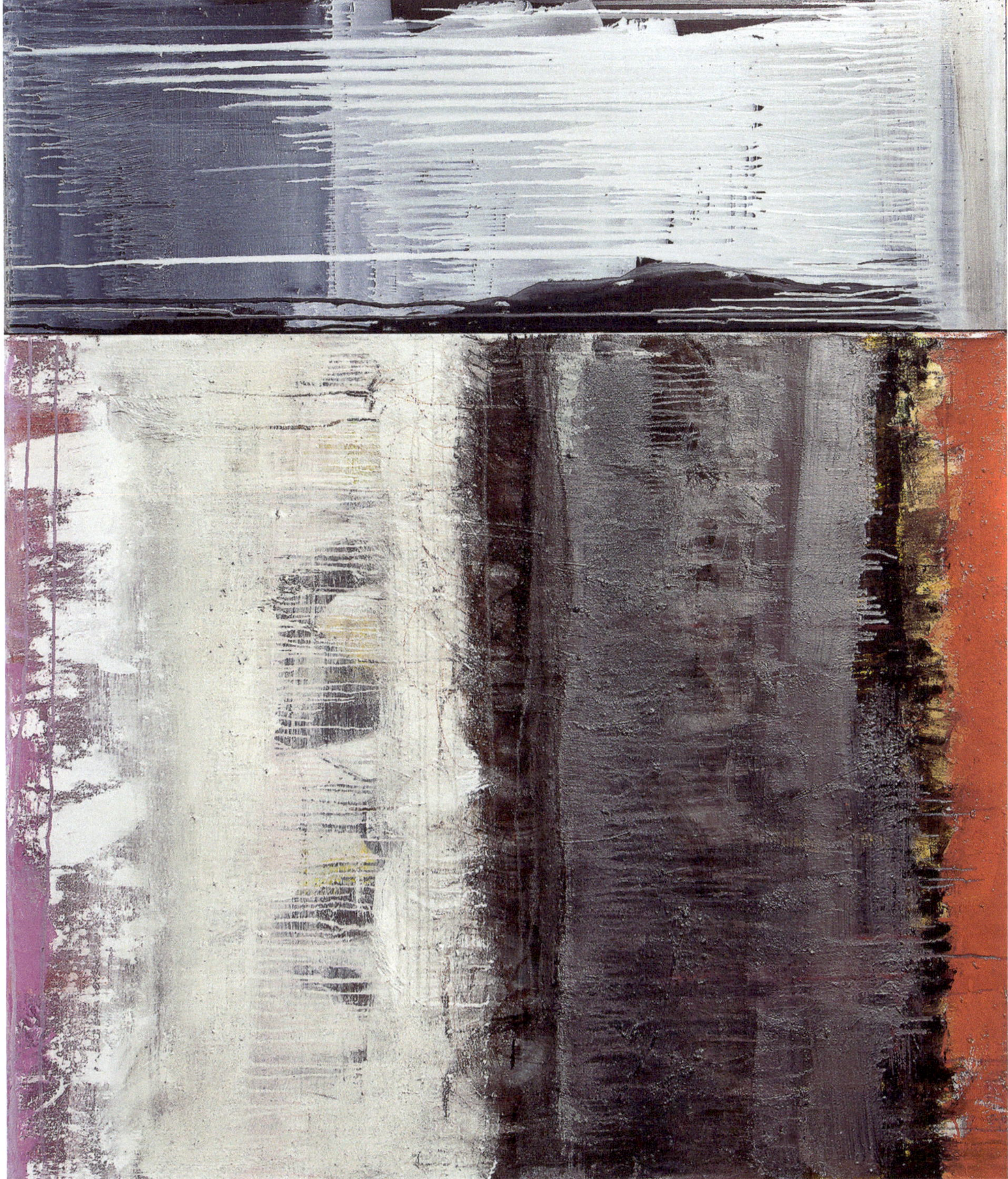

Treading hopes on lucid thoughts,
like *fara magnata*.
Horizons and butterfly patterns
are paths to nameless forms,
whole visions in black, white and silvers
combing themes to circular hope.

'Whirl Wind Motif'

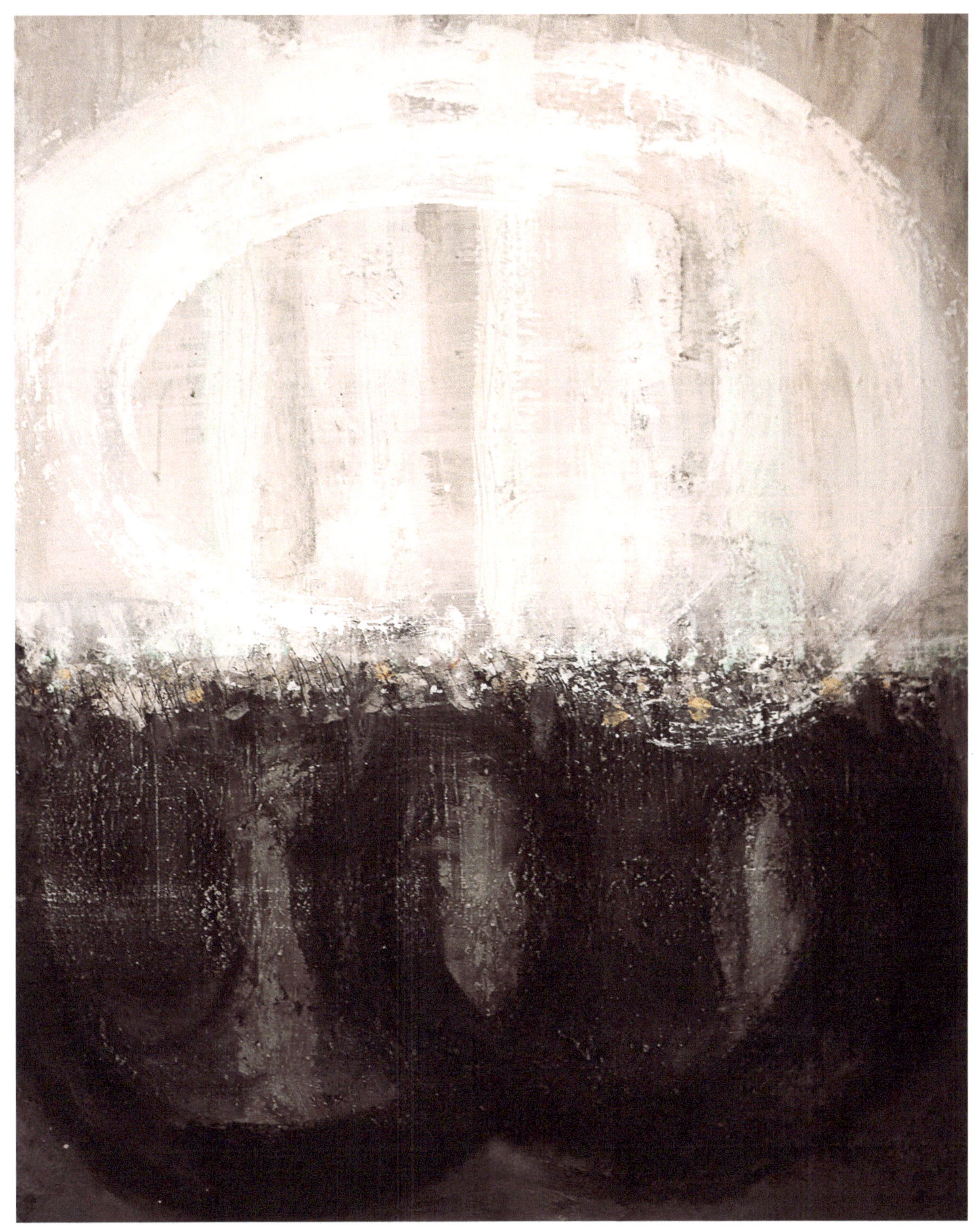

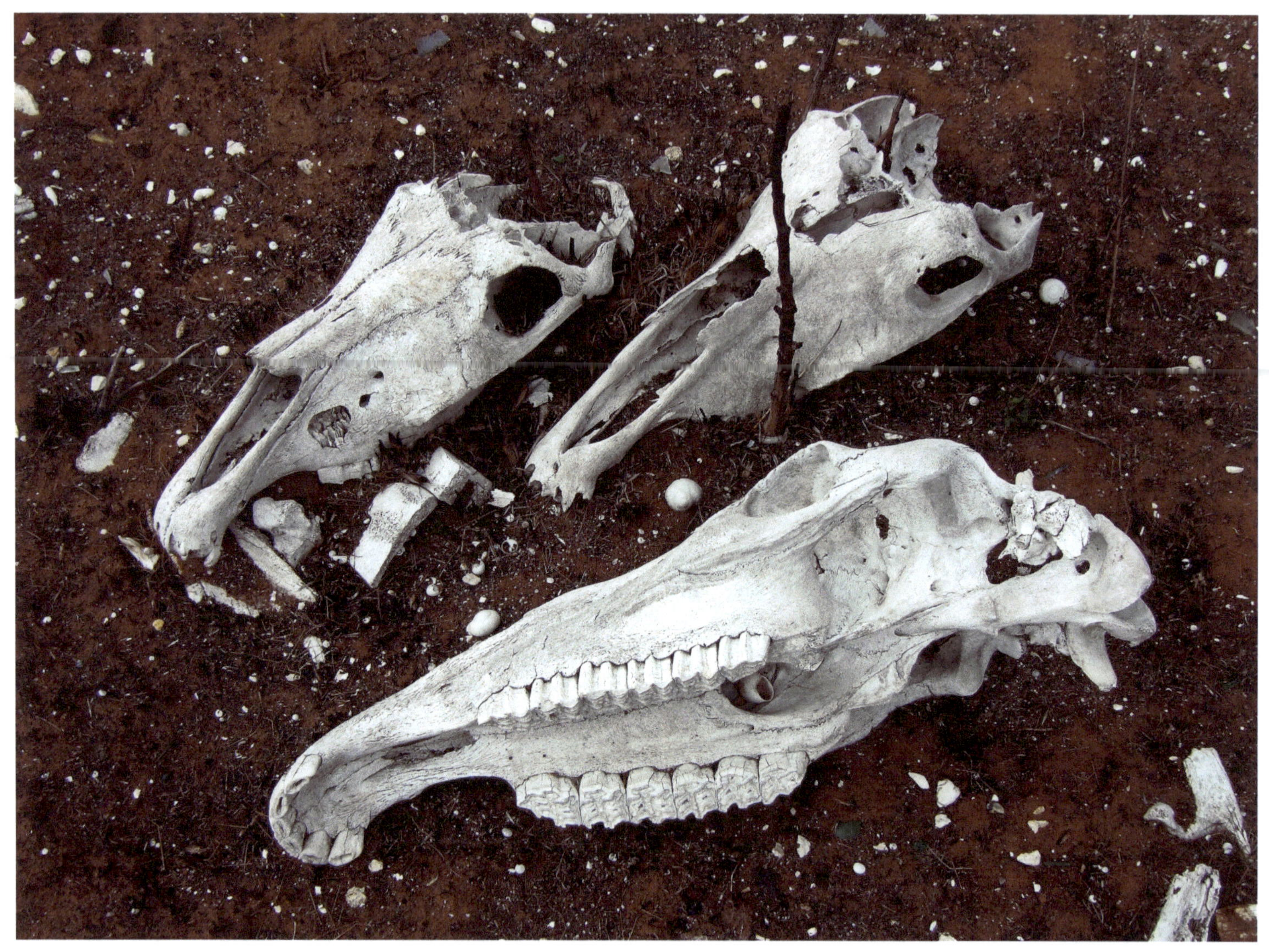

While on a three month art residency in Southern Italy, I bicycle to the next village for coffee, passing a field with old bones, bleached by time. The relics were beautiful and they wove their memory into the Italian series.

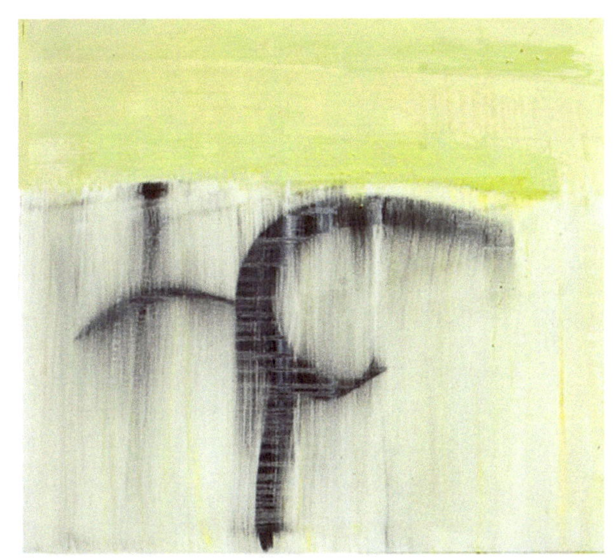

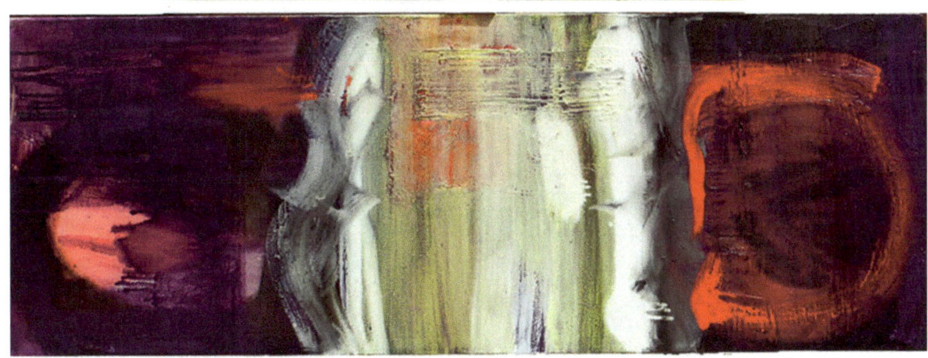

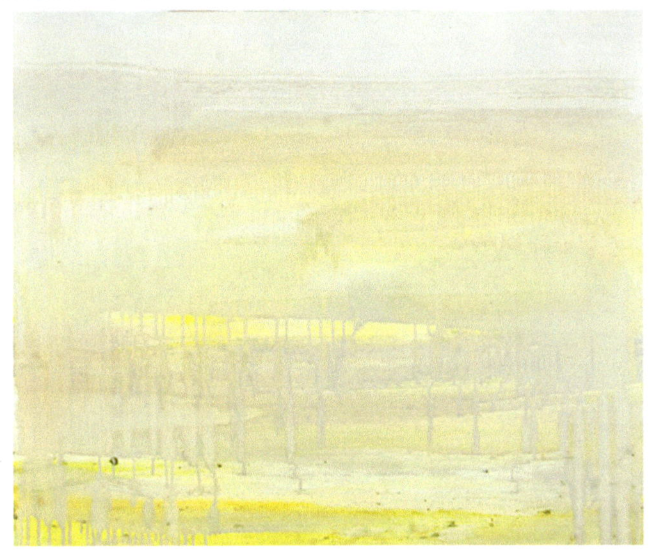

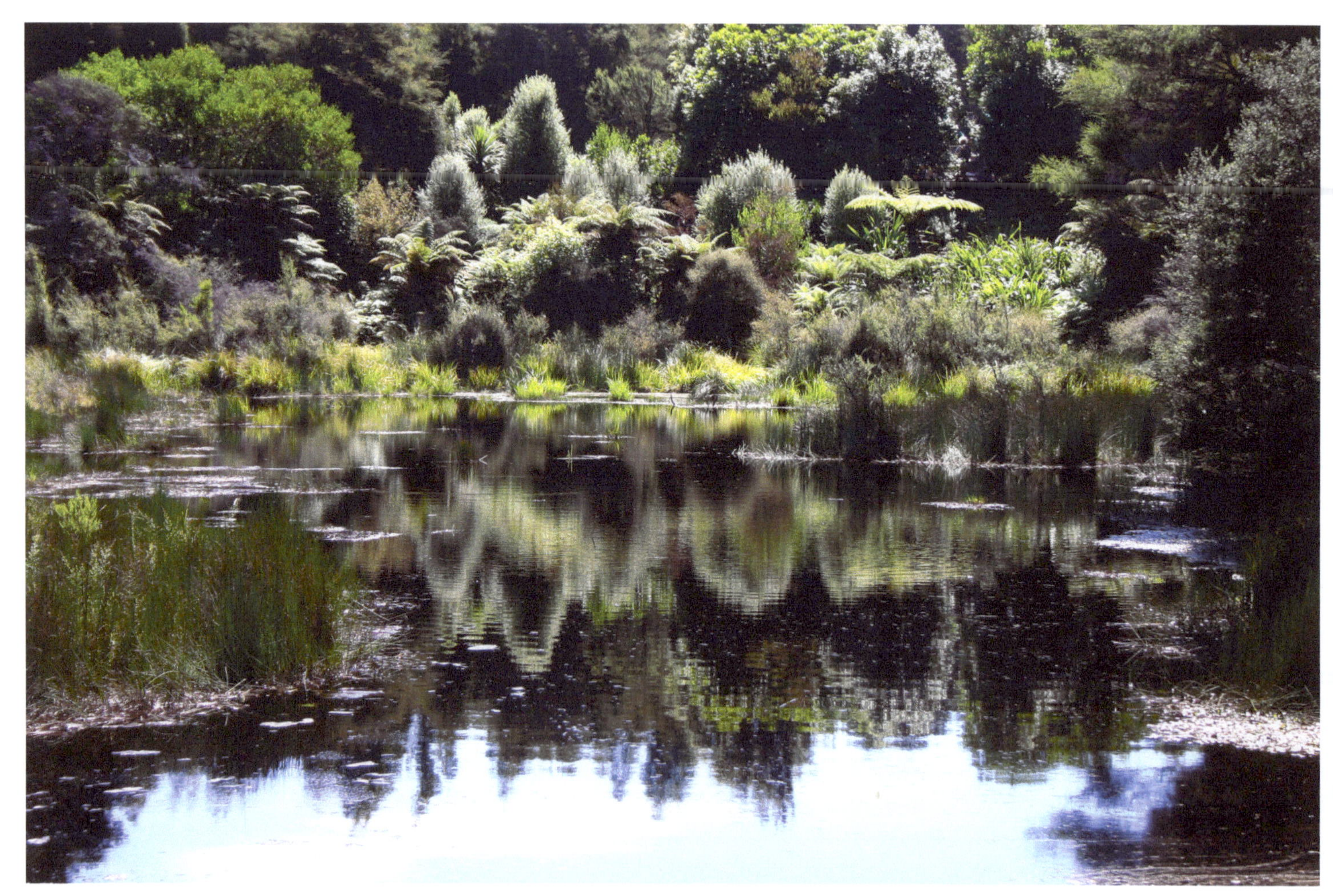

'Perch and Rest'

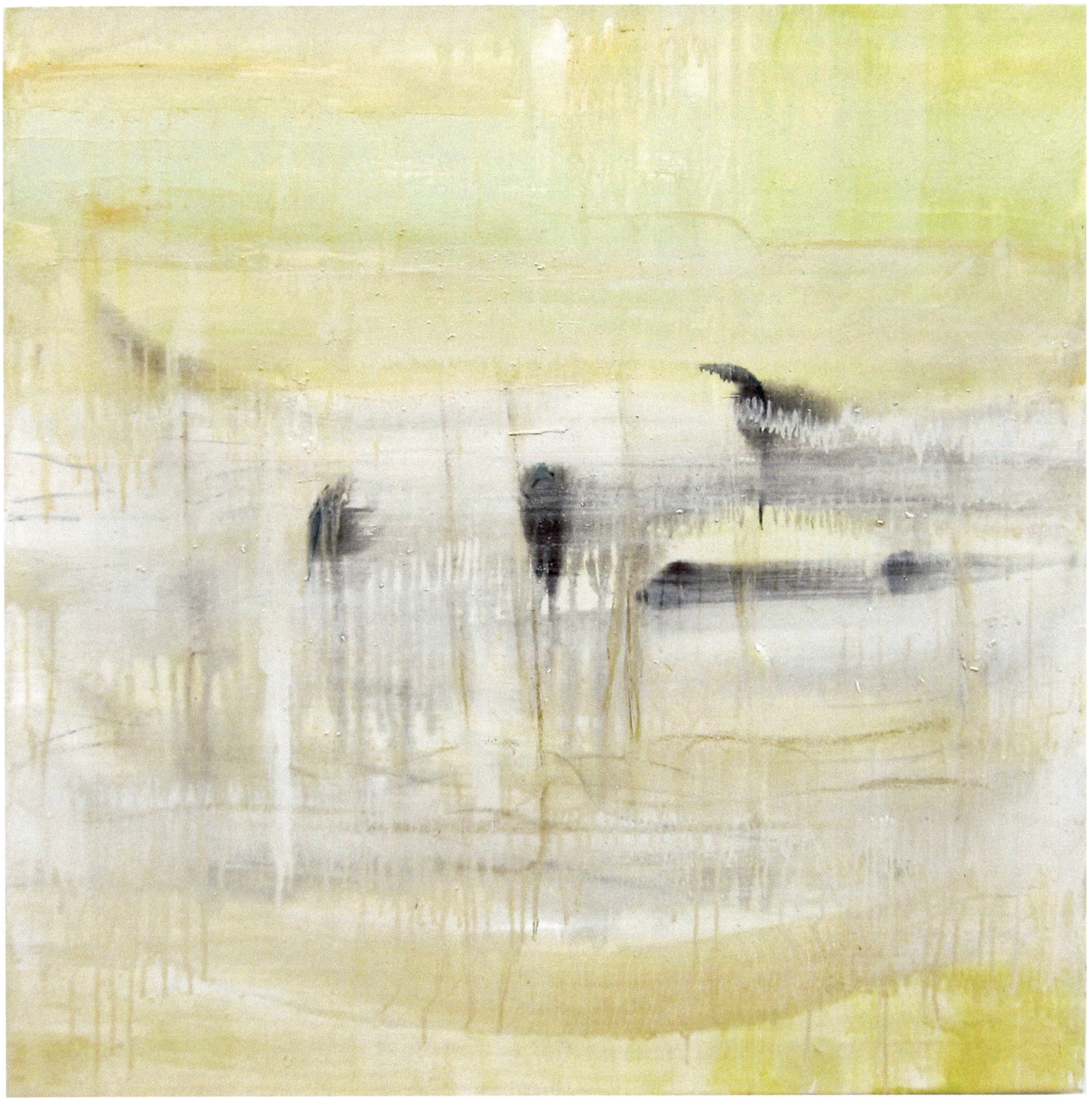

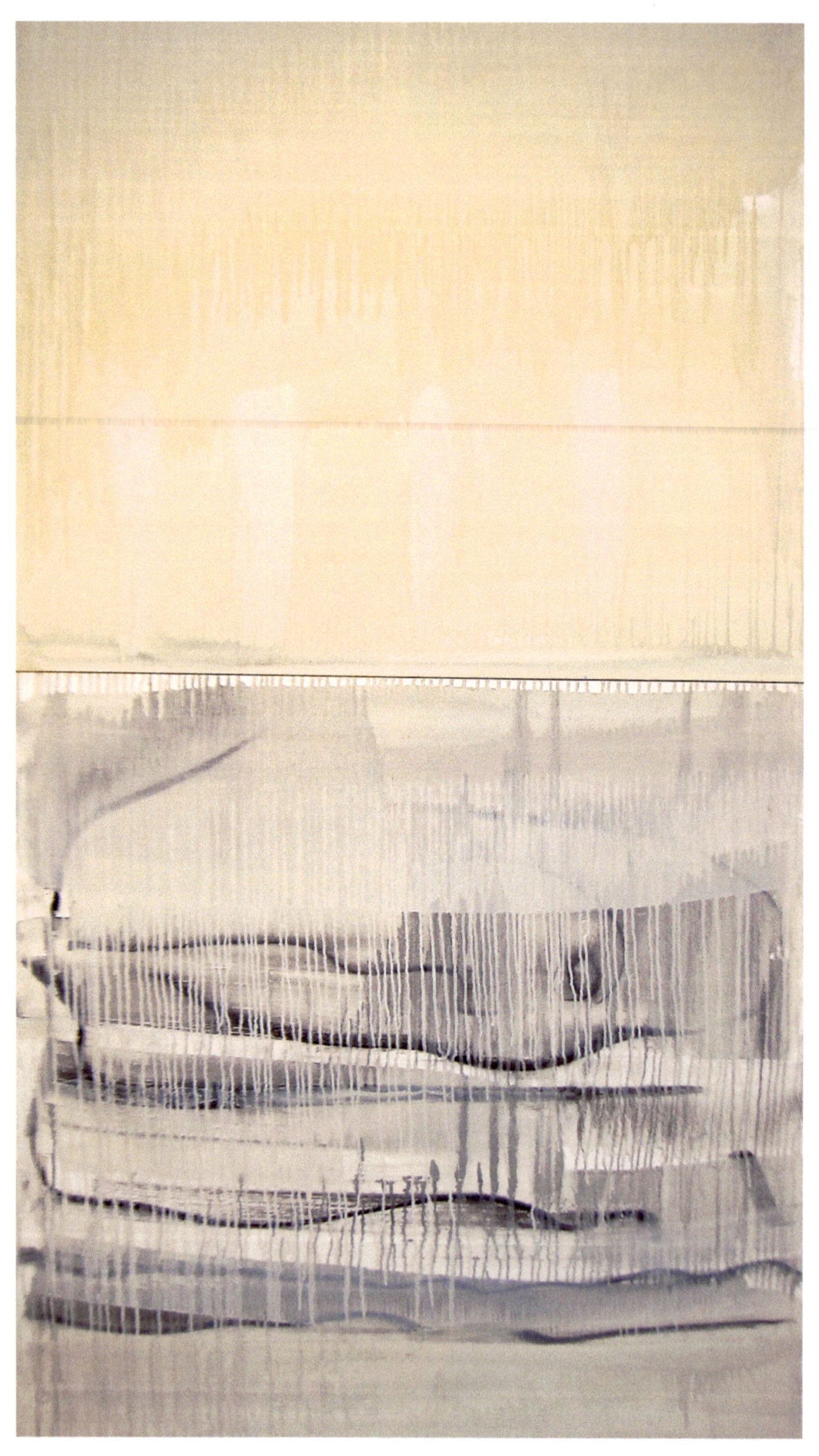

'White River Tundra'

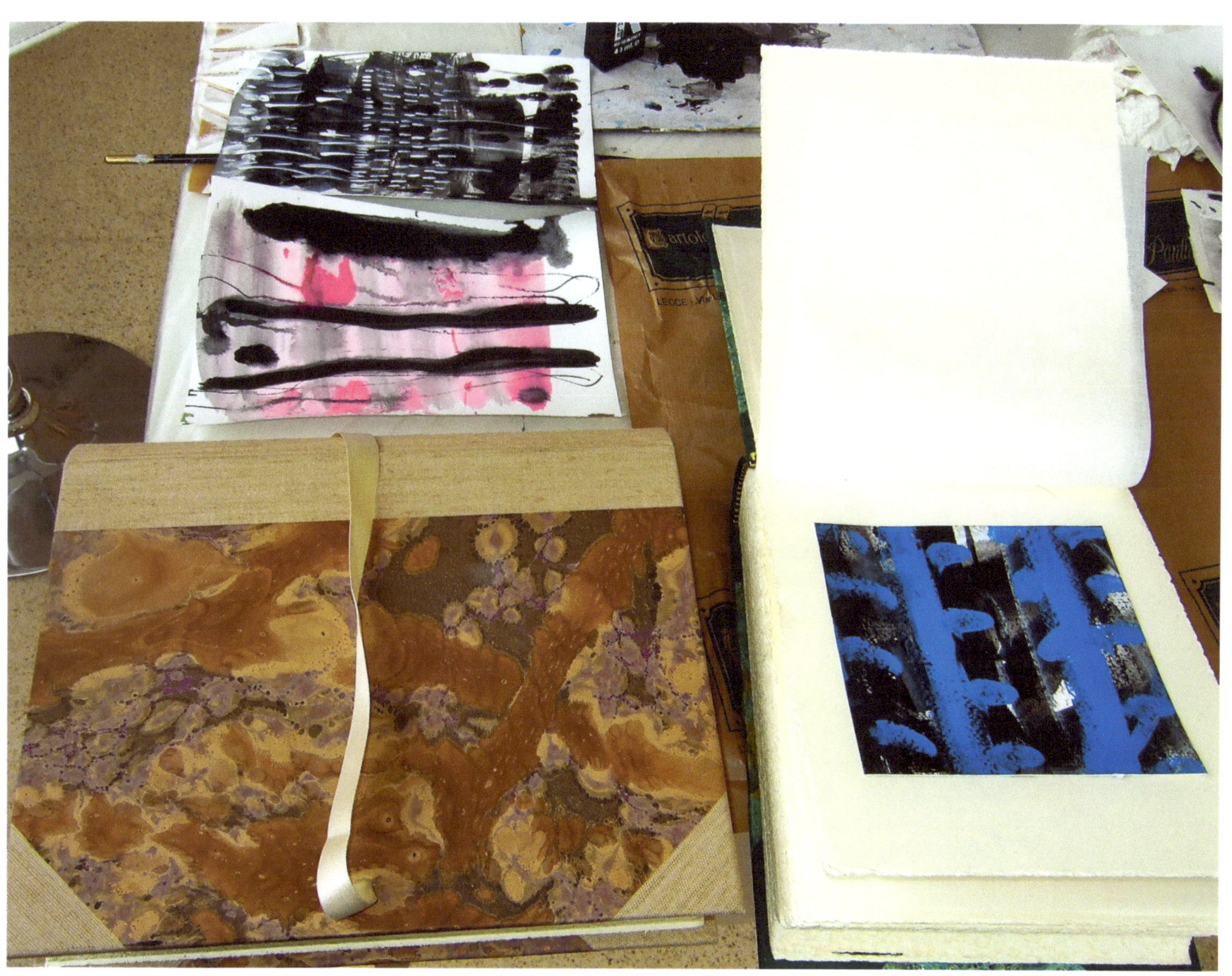

In Italy I created these ink narrative notebooks; ink on paper sketches in these beautifully handmade books I found in Lecce. This process of ink and gouache drawings influenced the charcoal under-drawings to many of the larger paintings.

'The physical beauty of her surrounds is a foundation of Lewenz's works and continues themes she has explored over the last twenty-five years. The rhythms of nature and the four elements (air, earth, fire and water) that are so dominant in her landscape recur throughout her works and reflect her deep connection to the natural environment. Yet, it is the fifth element - etheric or quintessence - that underpins her practice. The fluid, intuitive, ethereal and spiritual are conveyed through her artistic process, which involves combining and layering works using a selection of materials. This organic approach to art making evokes the lyricism of the natural world, whilst acknowledging the role of the random, haphazard and chaotic.'

bijoux eliot

'Chasm Between Sea and Meadow'

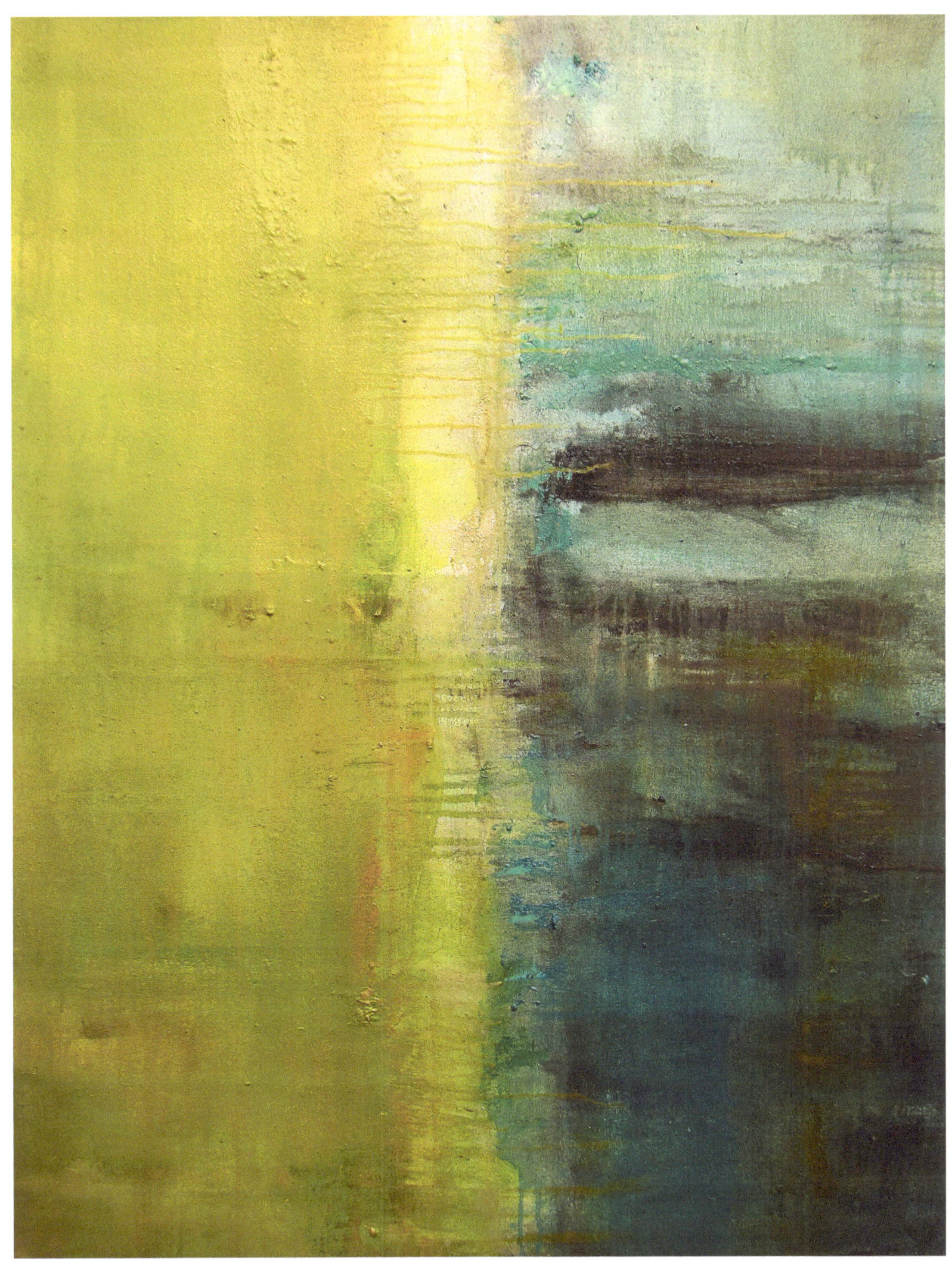

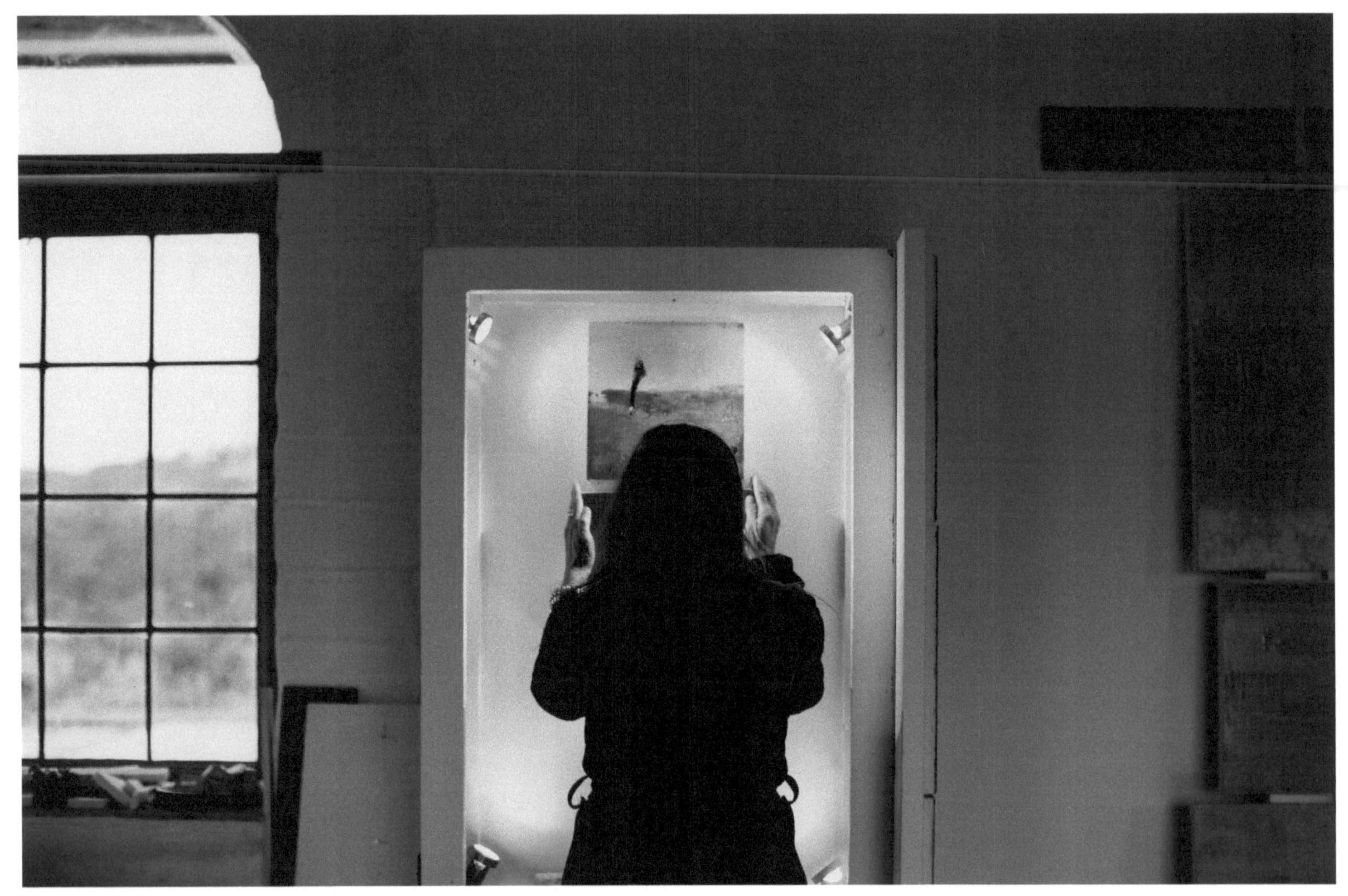

Photo: Amy Atkinson Photography

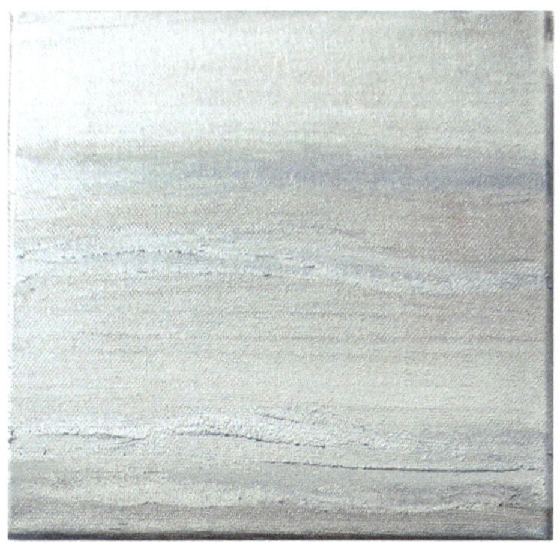

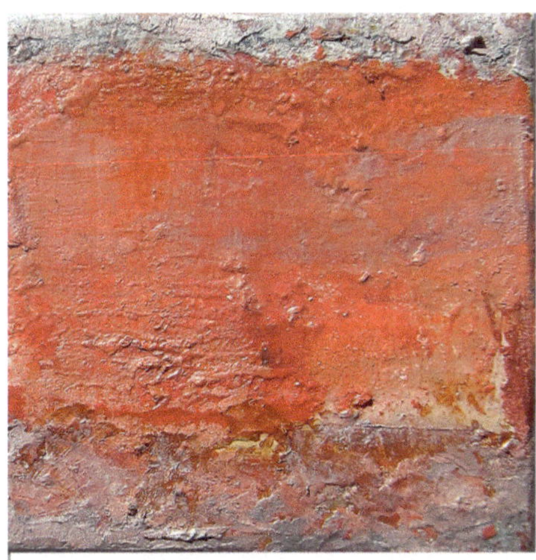

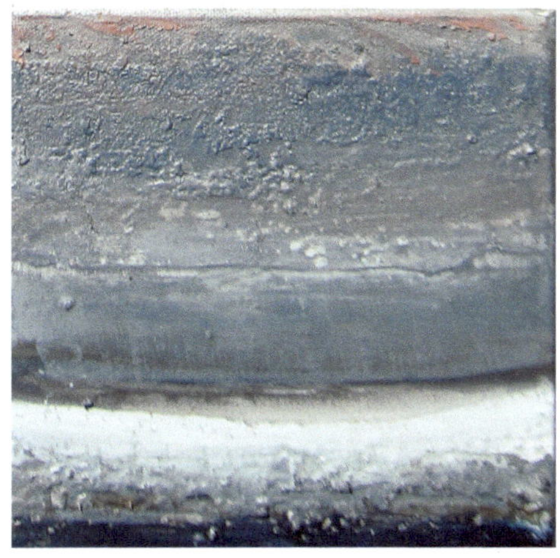

Dawn In Grey Beginnings

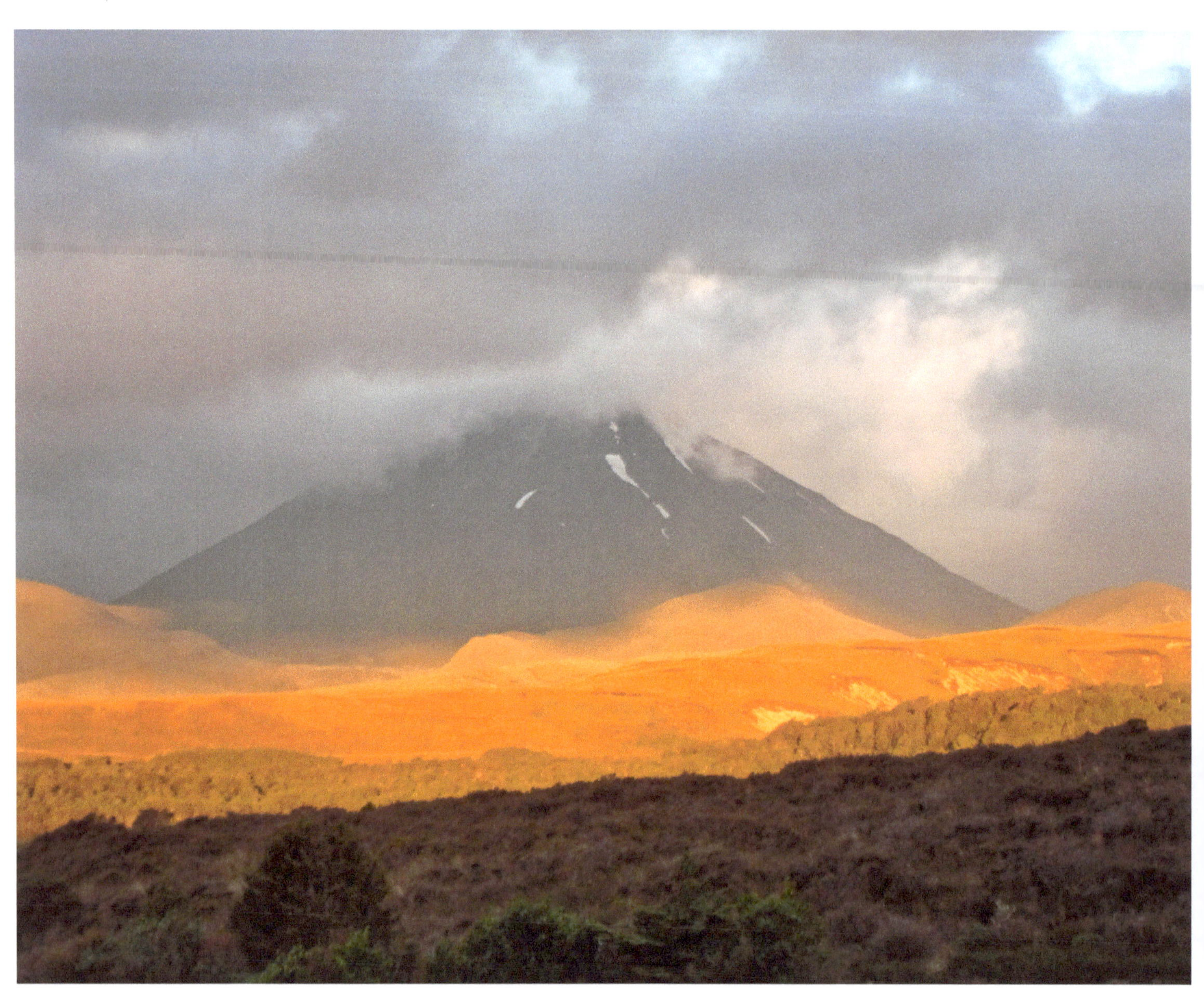

Mount Ngauruhoe

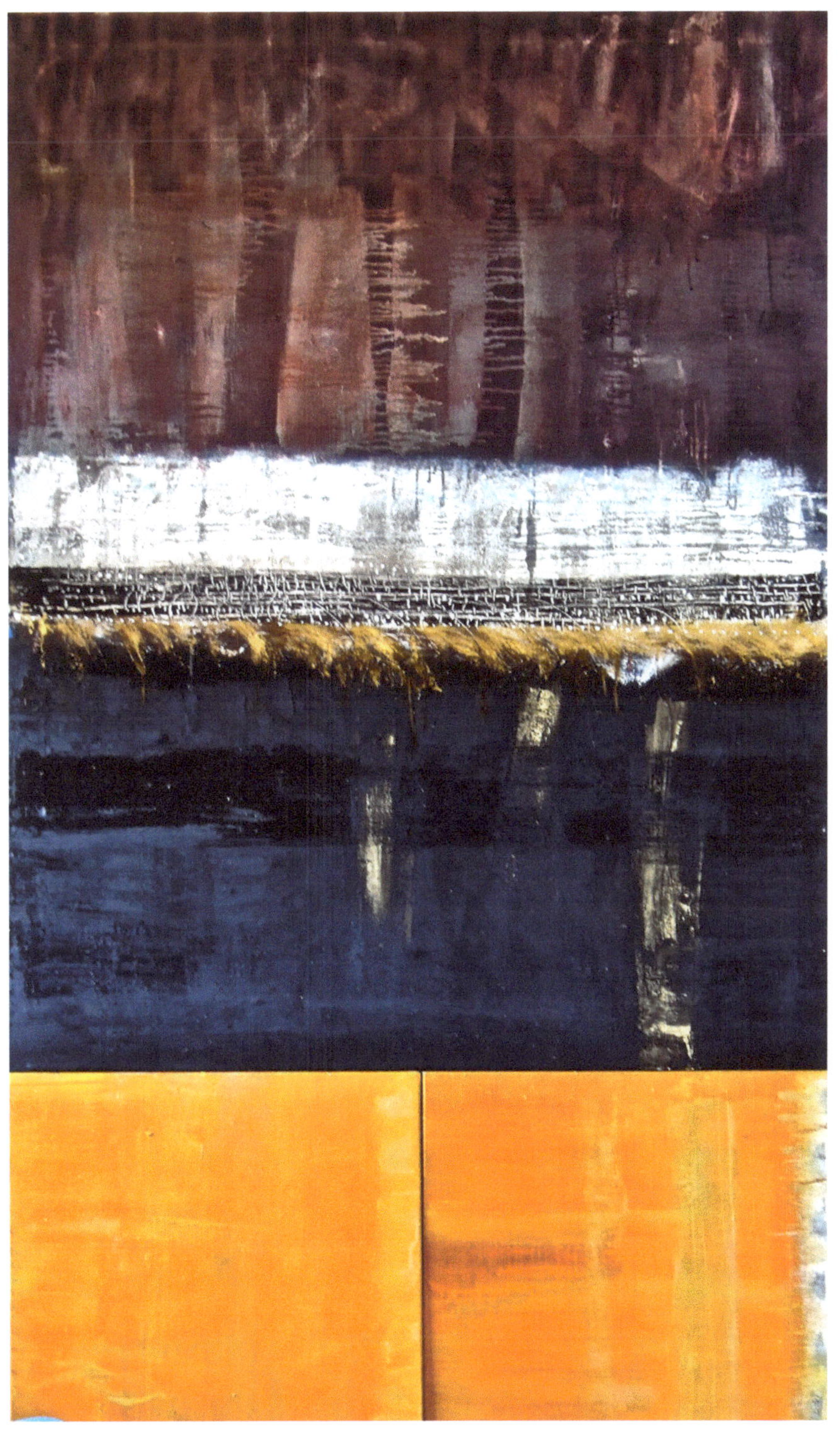

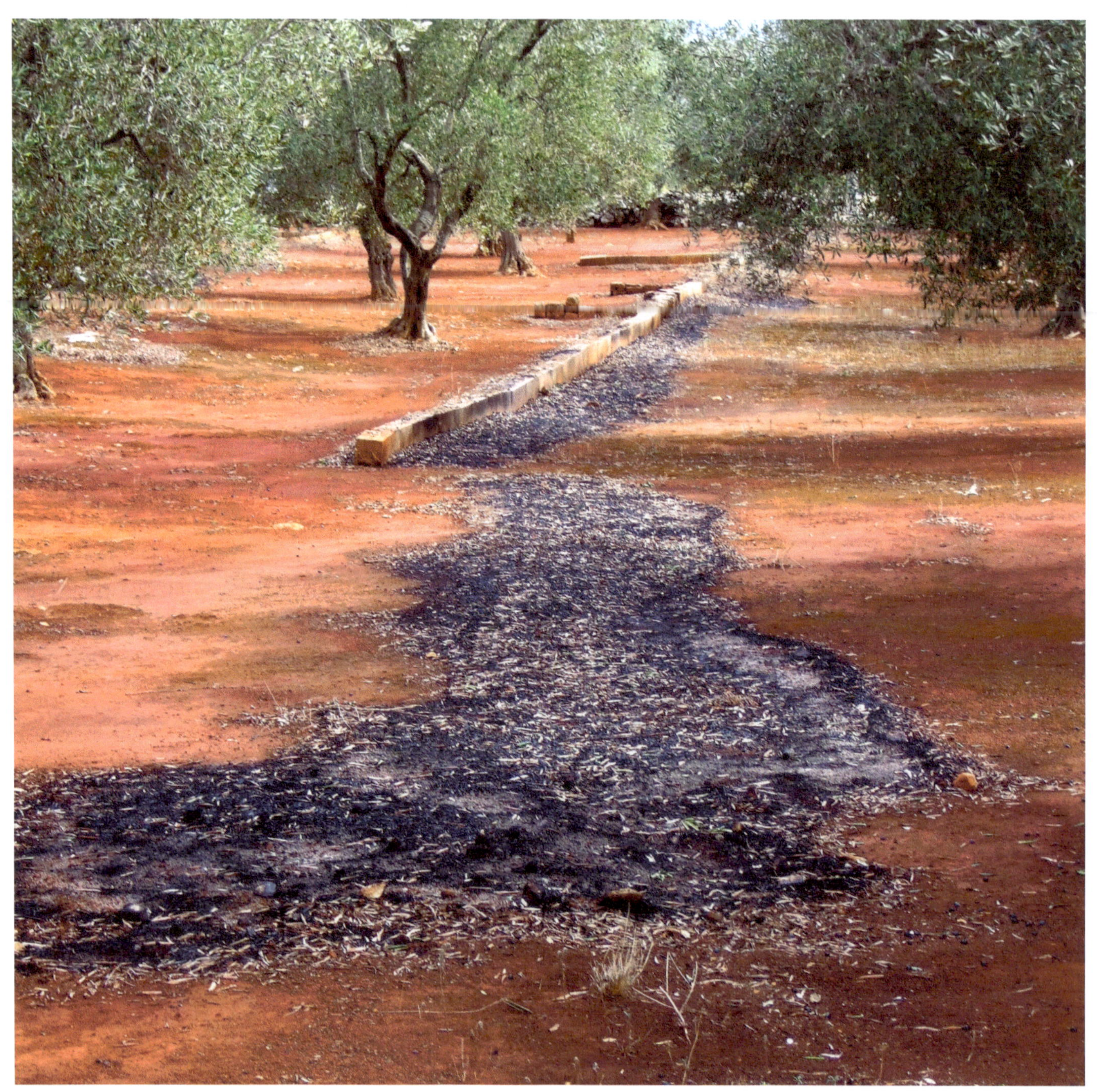

Autumn - Burning of the olive groves. Martignano Italy

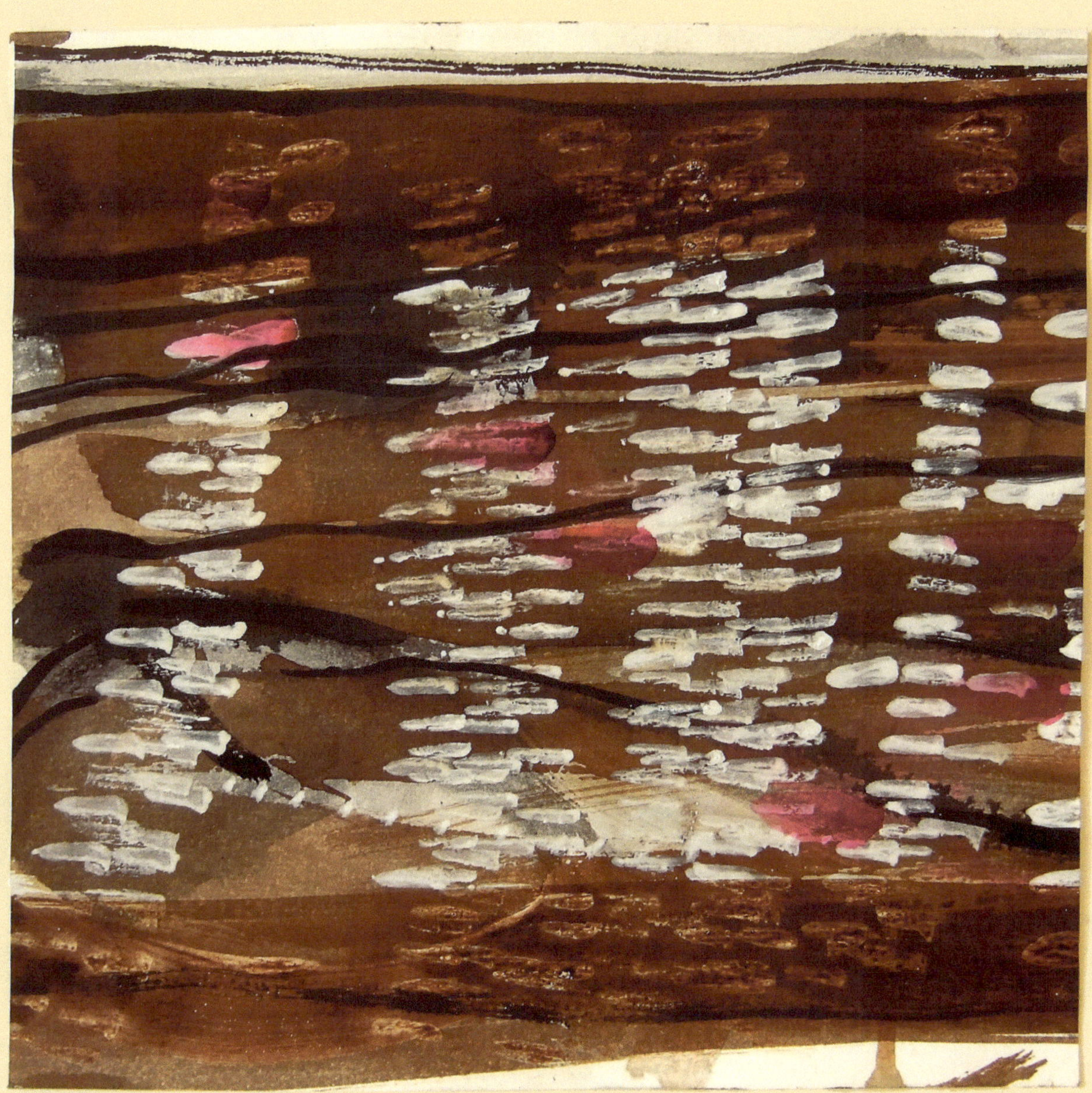

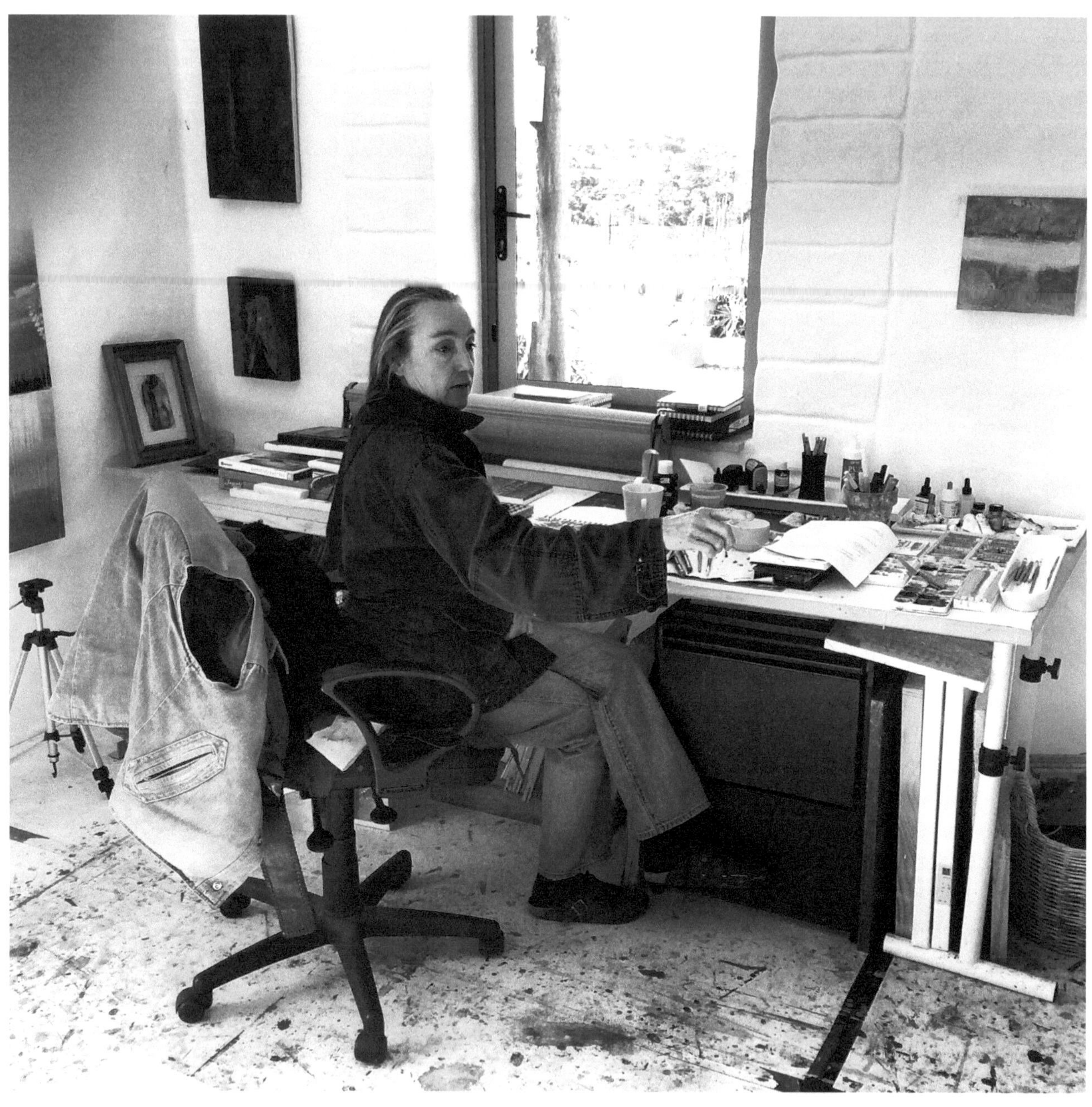

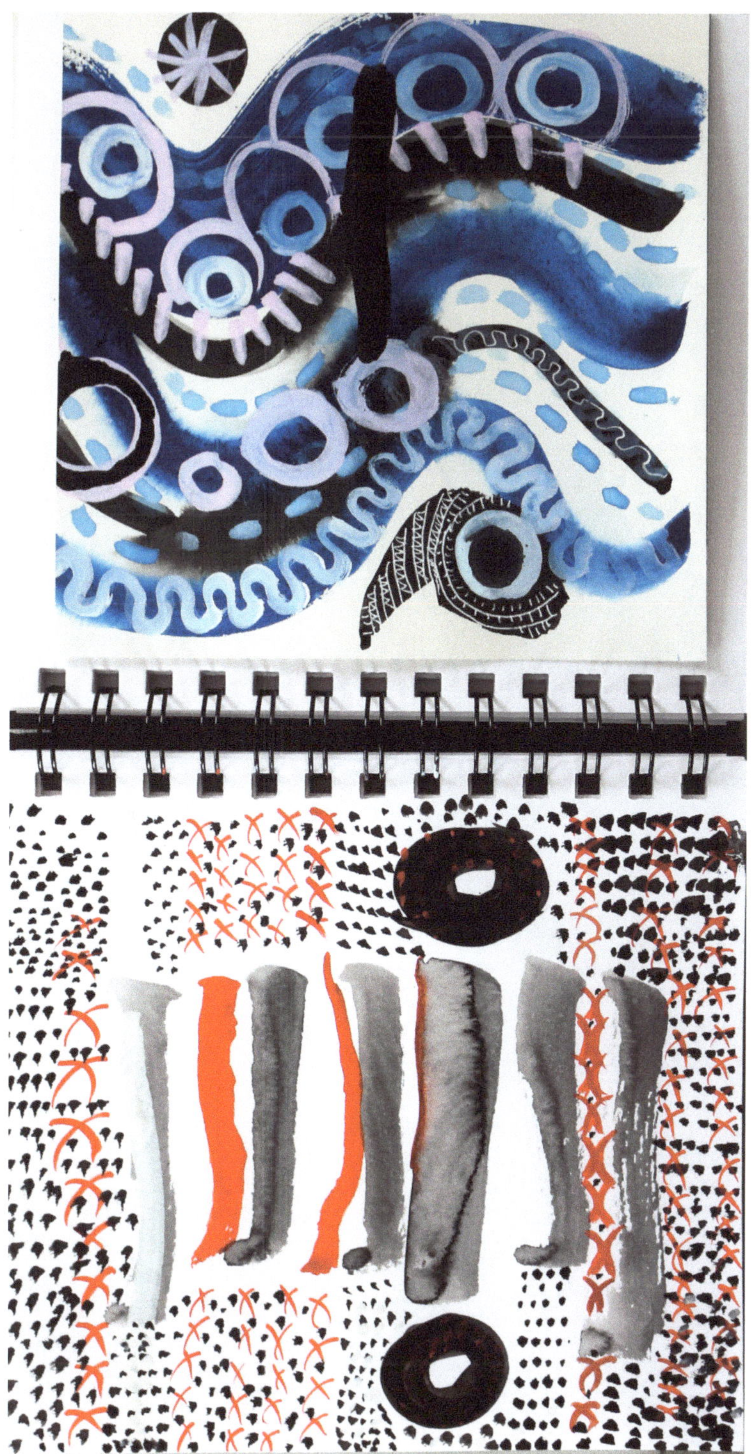

Studio journal

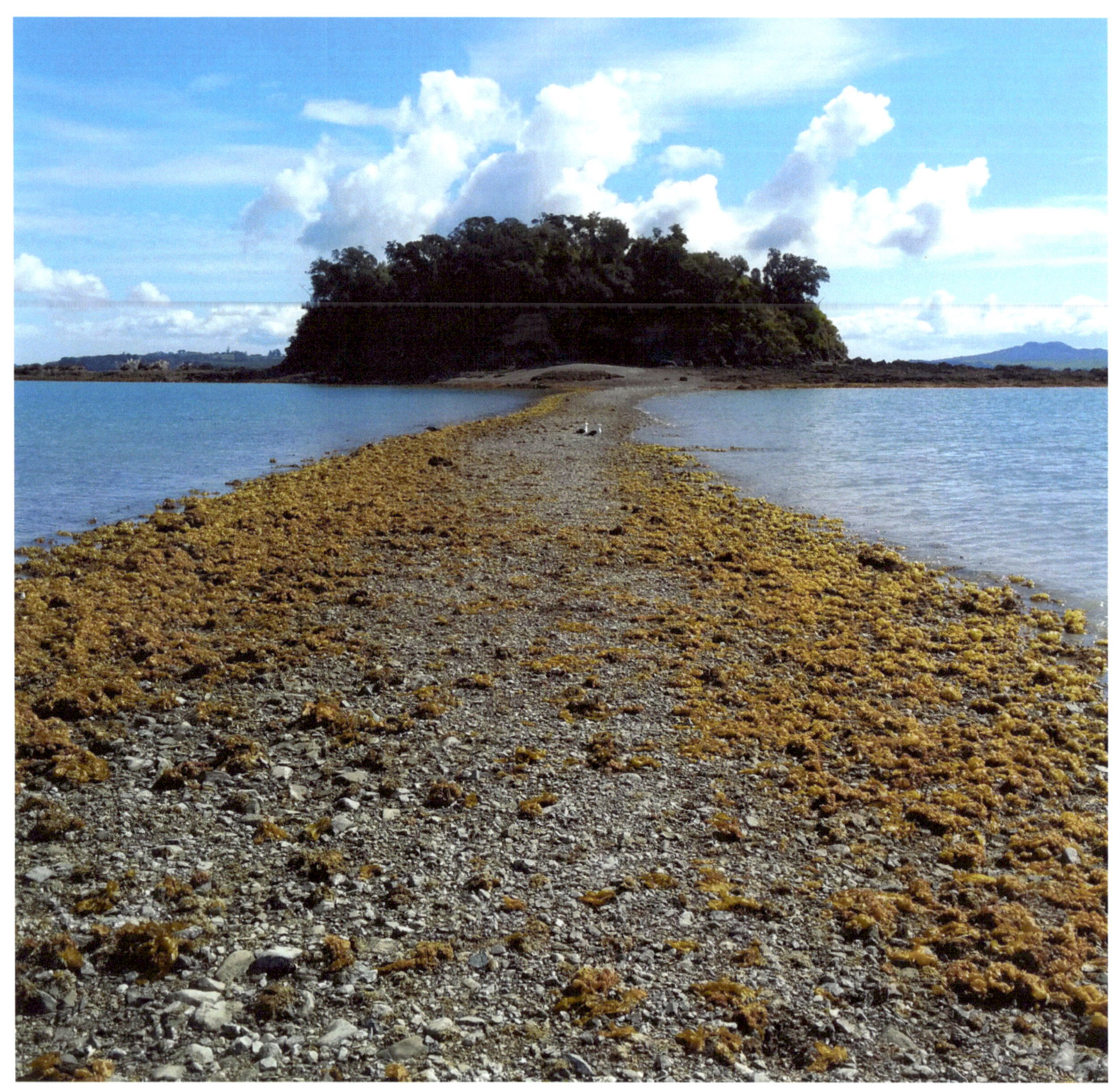

King Tide Low to Motukaha Island

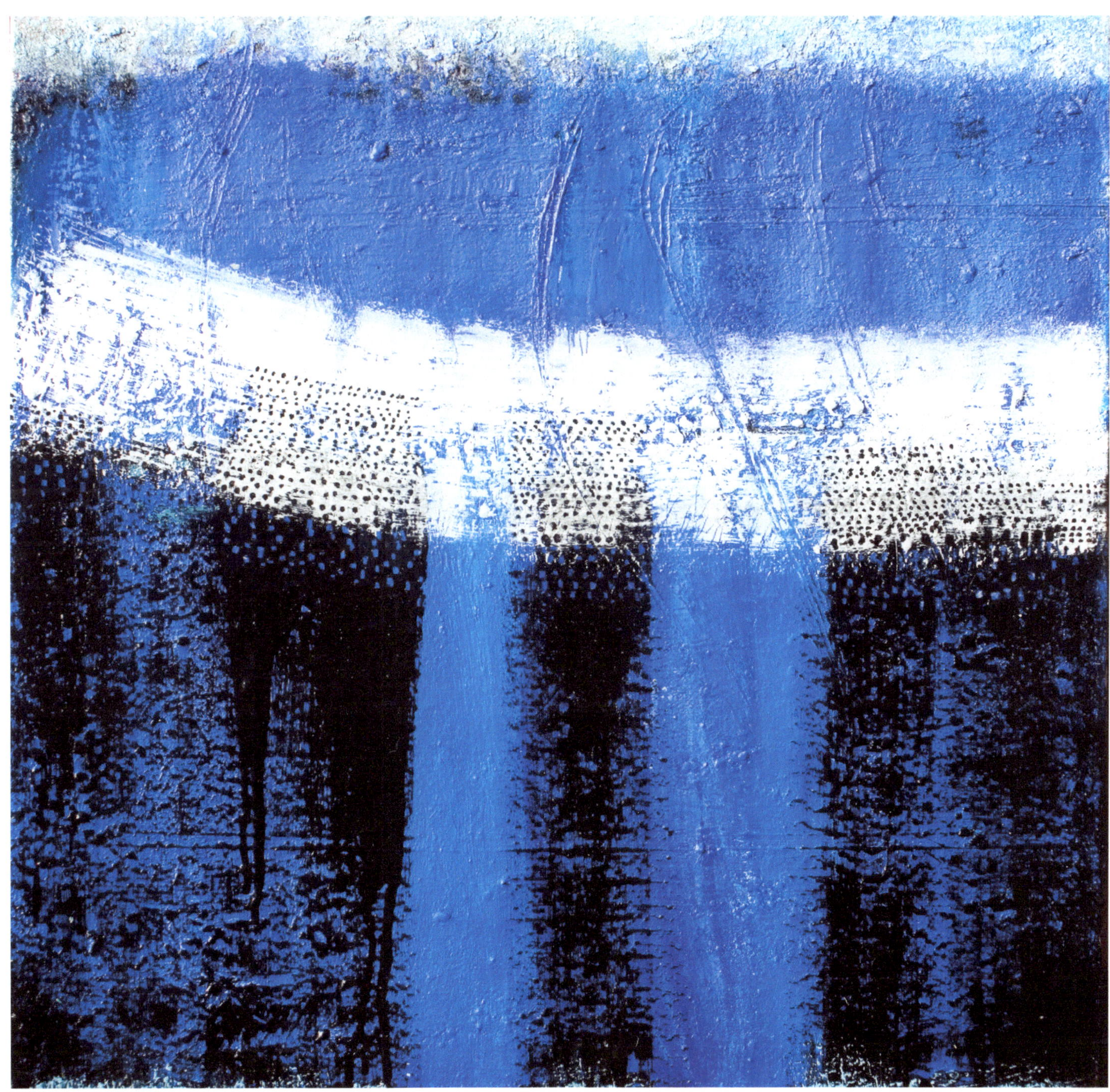

Ascending Shores

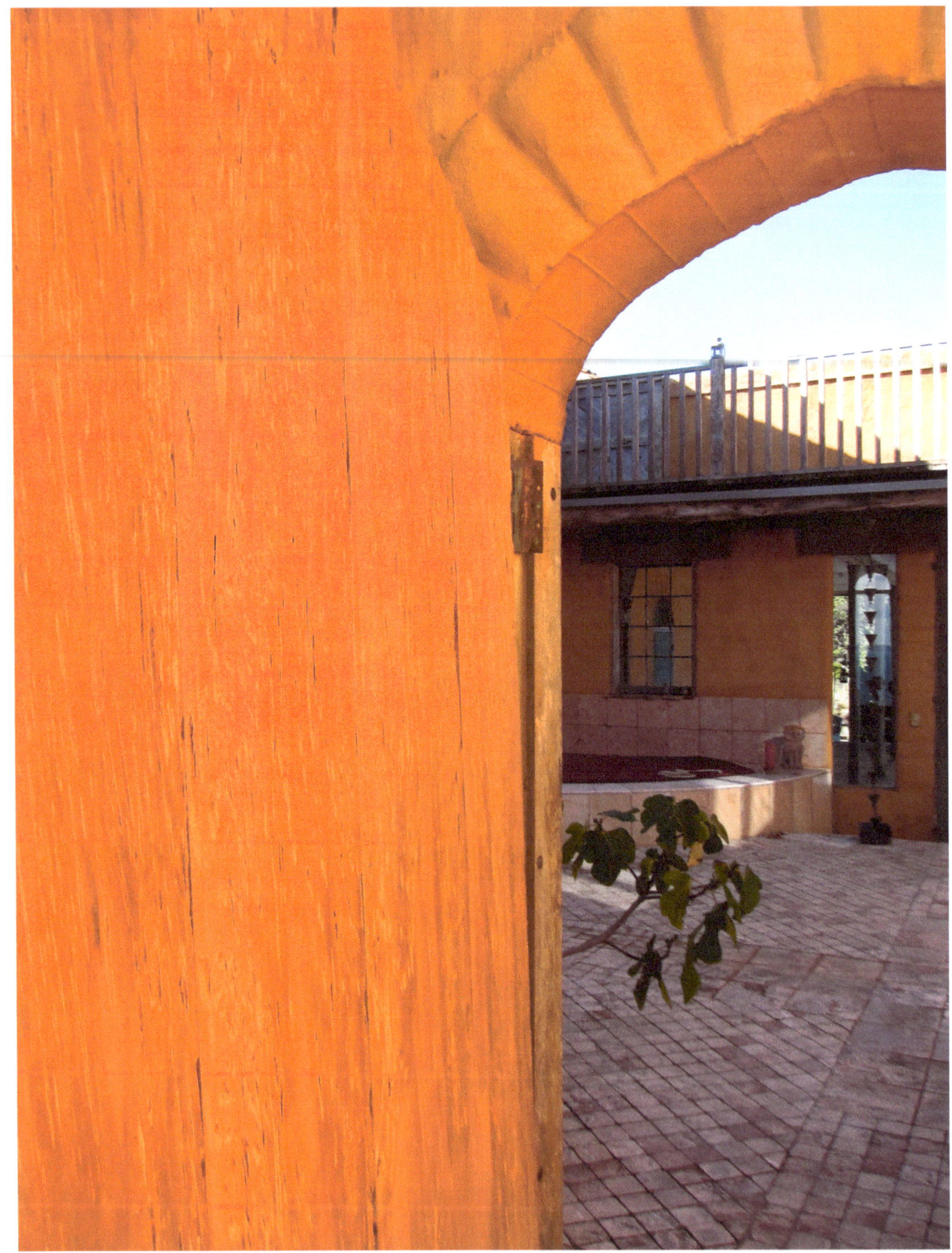

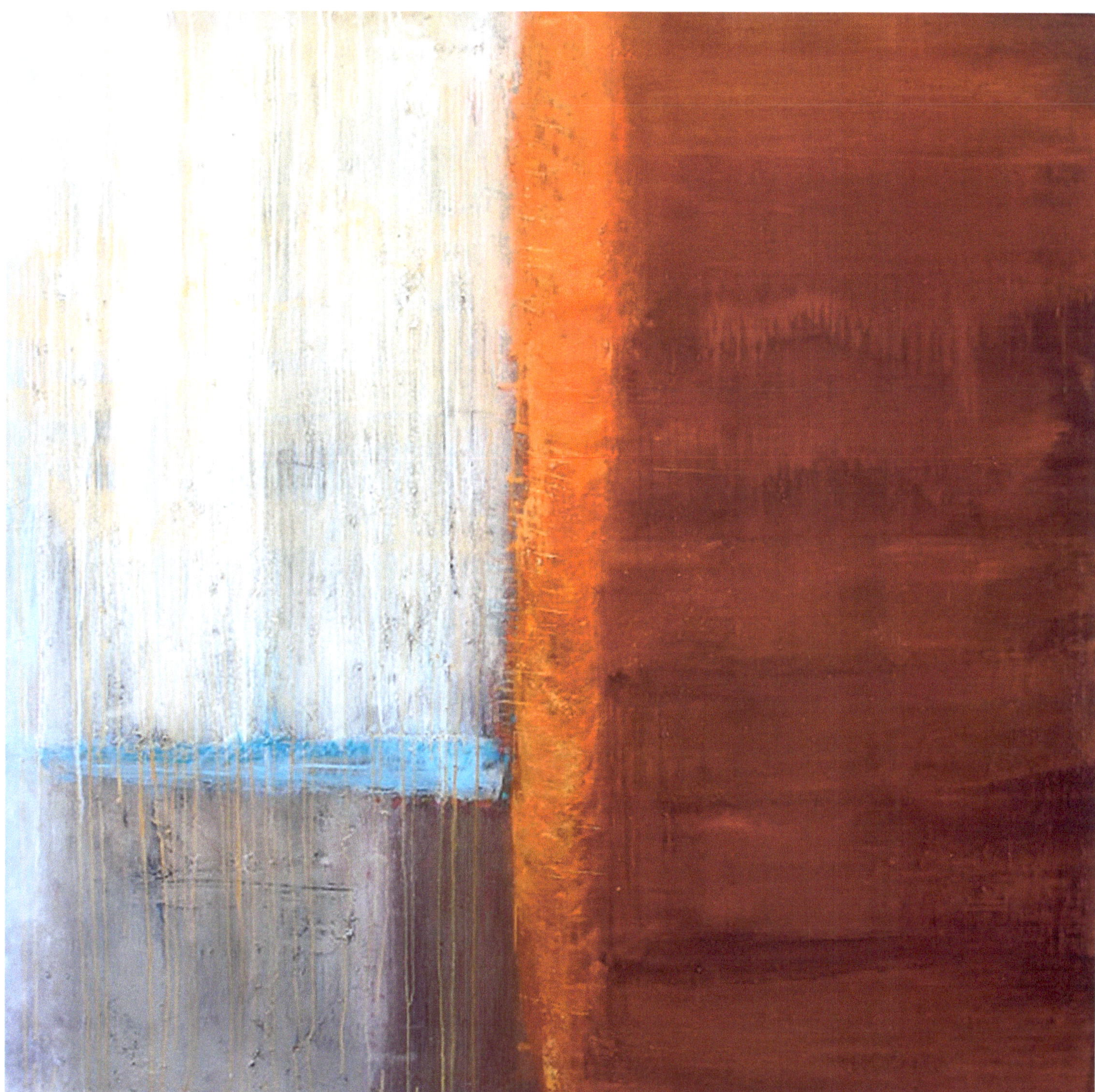

The ArtStay

A Passage and a Painting – Art Commissions

Gabriella offers you a beautiful and welcoming private sanctuary, to stay as her guest for in the guest cottage and an opportunity to focus on a commissioned work of art that captures the spirit of your journey or a special life event, or, if the right piece calls, to purchase a work of art from her studio gallery.

Experience a complete change of scenery and give yourself the space to reflect, restore and renew. Casale di Terra on Waiheke Island offers that getaway; a handmade Italianate earth-brick country house overlooking the sea in Church Bay. Your journey begins on the ferry, leaving from Auckland as you pass through the sacred volcano islands of the Hauraki Gulf, the fresh air washes your face, clears your mind and invigorates your soul. It's called ArtStay

artstay.com

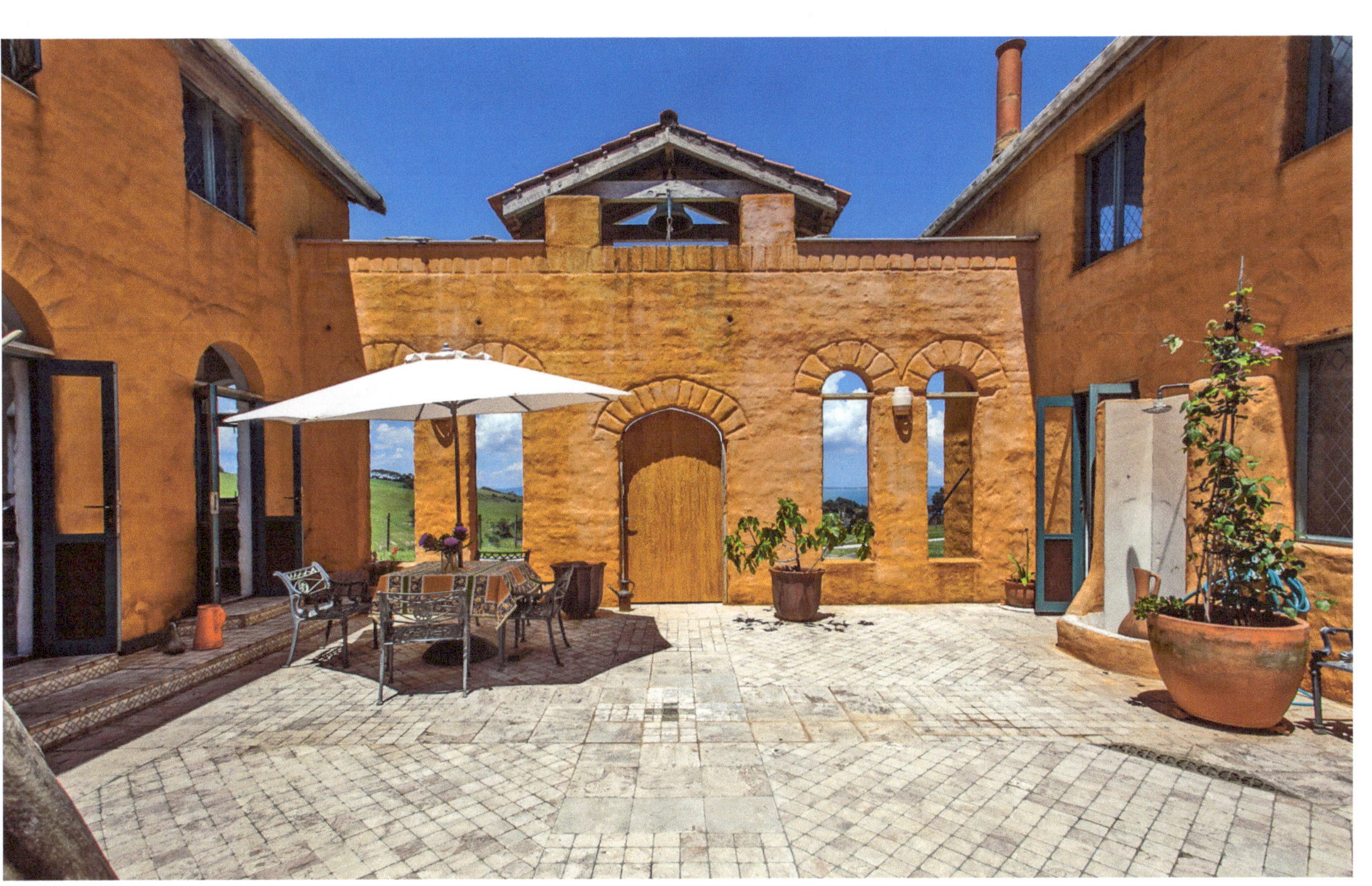

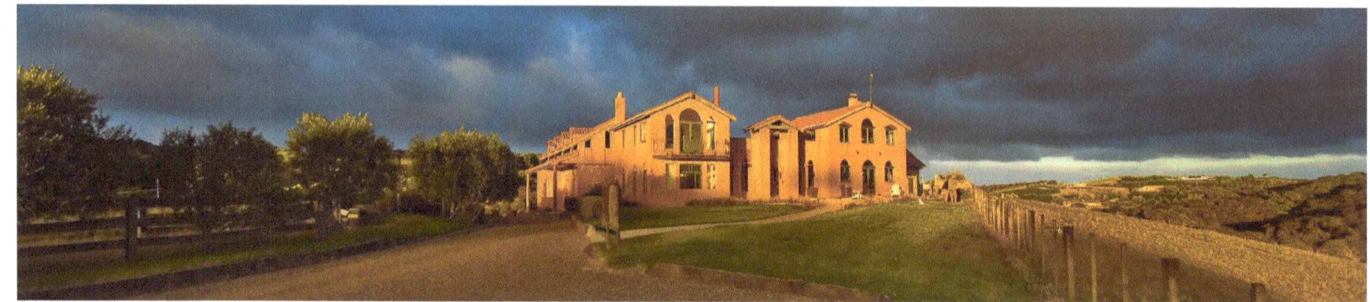

Gabriella Lewenz

is an American, born and raised in Greece and lived in Pakistan for a number of years before moving to the USA in her teens. In 1997 she migrated to New Zealand with her husband and daughter building Casale di Terra on Waiheke Island.

Gabriella works in handmade oils based on recipes of the old masters. She offers commissioned artworks on canvas, or on the three-paneled altarpiece – distinctive and does not require wall space. She's exhibited in galleries in NYC, Boston, New England, Italy and Auckland and now primarily sells her paintings from her studio gallery at Casale di Terra.

Her works are in private collections in the USA, Canada, UK, Austria, Sweden, Switzerland, Turkey, India, Hong Kong, Japan, Australia, Oceania and New Zealand

BFA Boston Museum School of Fine Arts and Tufts University

See lewenz.net

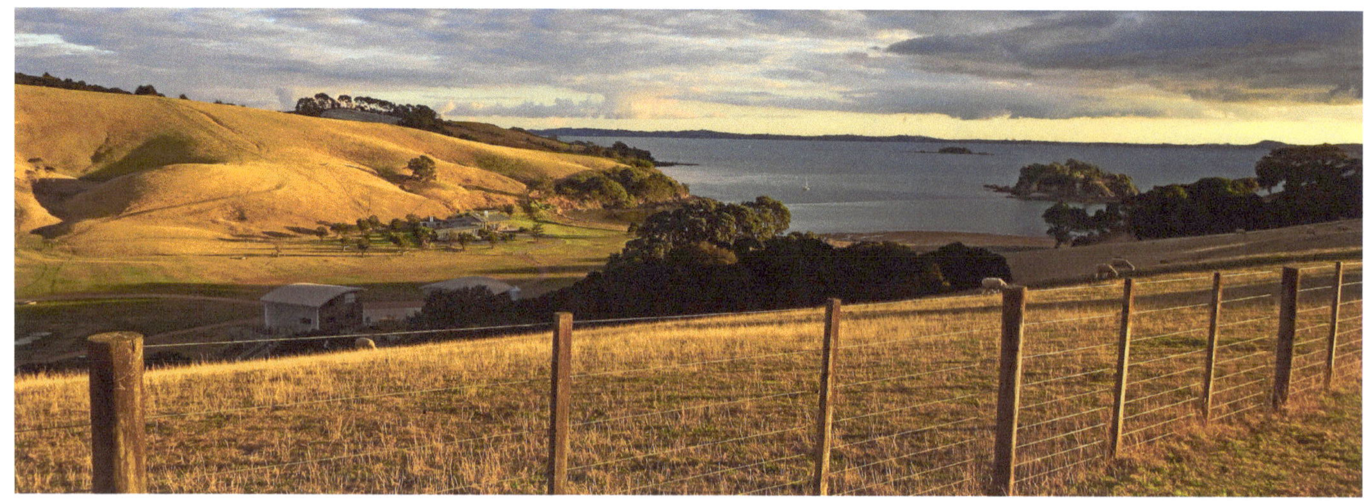